Belle M. Jewett

Singing on the Way

A Collection of Hymns and Tunes for Sunday Schools, Social Worship...

Belle M. Jewett

Singing on the Way
A Collection of Hymns and Tunes for Sunday Schools, Social Worship...

ISBN/EAN: 9783337228361

Printed in Europe, USA, Canada, Australia, Japan

Cover: Foto ©Thomas Meinert / pixelio.de

More available books at **www.hansebooks.com**

SINGING ON THE WAY.

A COLLECTION OF

HYMNS AND TUNES

FOR

SUNDAY SCHOOLS,

Social Worship and Congregations.

COMPILED AND ARRANGED BY

MRS. BELLE M. JEWETT,

NEW YORK CITY;

ASSISTED BY

DR. J. P. HOLBROOK,

Author of "Worship in Song," "Quartet and Chorus Choir," &o.

———————

PUBLISHED BY

DITSON & CO.,

Boston, New York, and Philadelphia.

ANNOUNCEMENT.

This Book is offered to the public with the diffidence natural to a first venture. That diffidence is increased by the fact that so few of my sex have attempted the compilation of a music book. Had I been unaided I should have hesitated; but fortunately, my old time musical preceptor, Dr. Jos. P. Holbrook, came to my assistance, with his experience as a compiler and composer, adding several of his own compositions never before published. This has given me a confidence which I otherwise lacked, and emboldens me to submit "*Singing on the Way*," unhesitatingly, to the public, and to solicit for the work a share of that generous consideration so largely bestowed by Sunday-school officials, upon collections of sacred songs made in the special interest of children.

I desire here to gratefully express thanks for assistance rendered, and for kind permission to use many very excellent and popular pieces, to the Rev. E. P. Parker, D.D., author of the S. S. Hymnal, Prof. Jas. H. Fillmore, of Cincinnati, Mess. Jno. Church & Co., Cincinnati, Mess. S. Brainard, Sons & Co., of Cleveland, Dr. Geo. F. Root, and Prof. T. Martin Towne, also Mess. Towne & Stilkman, of Chicago, Mr. H. C. Camp, Mr. F. L. Armstrong, Mess. A. S. Barnes & Co., and Mess. O. Ditson & Co.

BELLE M. JEWETT,
NEW YORK.

SINGING ON THE WAY.

OPENING OF SCHOOL.

THE LORD'S PRAYER.

TALLIS.

Our Father, which art in Heaven, hallowed | be Thy | Name: ‖ Thy kingdom
come: Thy will be done in | earth· as it | is in | Heaven.
Give us this day our | daily | bread; ‖ And forgive us our debts as | we for- |
give our | debtors;
And lead us not into temptation, but deliver | us from | evil; ‖ For Thine is
the kingdom, and the power, and the | glory· for- | ever. ·A- | men.

GLORIA PATRI.*

Glo - ry be to the Fa - ther, and to the Son, and to the

Ho - ly Ghost; As it was in the be - gin - ning, is

now, and ev - er shall be, world without end. A - men. A - men.

*Used by permission of O. Ditson & Co.

(3)

VENITE EXULTEMUS DOMINO.

Ps. xcv.

1 O come, let us sing un- | to the | Lord;
Let us heartily rejoice in the | strength of | our sal- | vation.

2 Let us come before His presence | with thanks- | giving;
And show ourselves | glad in | Him with | psalms.

3 For the Lord is a | great — | God;
And a great | King a- | bove all | gods.

4 In His hands are all the corners | of the | earth,
And the strength of the | hills is | His — | also.

5 The sea is His, | and He | made it;
And His hands pre- | pared the | dry — | land.

6 O come, let us worship, | and fall | down;
And kneel be- | fore the | Lord, our | Maker:

7 For He is the | Lord our | God;
And we are the people of His pasture, and the | sheep of | His — | hand.

8 O worship the Lord in the | beauty of | holiness;
Let the whole earth | stand in | awe of | Him:

9 For He cometh, for He cometh, to | judge the | earth;
And with righteousness to judge the world, and the | people | with His | truth.

Glory be to the Father, and | to the | Son,
And | to the | Holy | Ghost;
As it was in the beginning, is now, and | ever | shall be,
World | without | end. A- | men.

Glory be to | God on | high: ‖ and on earth | peace, good | will towards | men.
We praise Thee, we bless Thee, we | worship | Thee: ‖ we glorify Thee, we give
thanks to | Thee for | Thy great | glory.

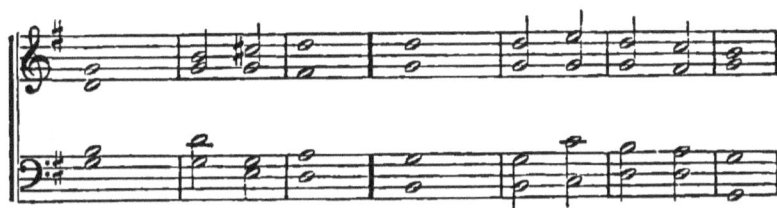

O Lord God, | Heavenly | King: ‖ God the | Father | Al — | mighty!
O Lord, the only-begotten Son | Jesus | Christ: ‖ O Lord God, Lamb of God, |
Son — | of the | Father,

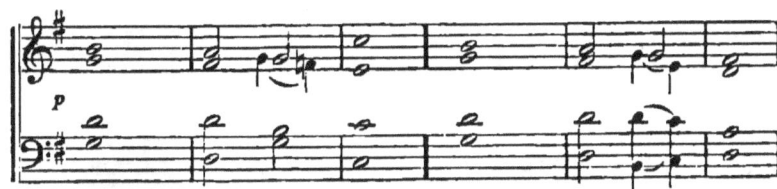

That takest away the | sins of the | world, ‖ have mercy | upon | us.
Thou that takest away the | sins of the | world, ‖ have mercy | upon | us.
Thou that takest away the | sins of the | world, ‖ re- | ceive our | prayer.
Thou that sittest at the right hand of | God the | Father, ‖ have mercy | upon | us.

A - men.

For Thou only | art — | holy: ‖ Thou | only | art the | Lord.
Thou only, O Christ, with the | Holy | Ghost, ‖ art most high in the | glory of |
God the | Father. ‖ A- | men.

Let the words of my mouth, and the med - i - ta - tion of my

heart, be ac - cept - a - ble in thy sight, O Lord, my

strength, and my Re - deem - er,   O Lord, my strength, O Lord, my

strength, and my Re - deem - er,   O Lord, ... my

strength, O Lord, my strength, and my Re - deem - er.

A - men.

Ps. xxiii.

1 The Lord is my Shepherd; I | shall not | want. ‖ He maketh me to lie down in green pastures; He leadeth me beside the | still — | waters.

2 He restoreth my soul; He leadeth me in the paths of righteousness for His | name's — | sake. ‖ Yea, though I walk through the valley of the shadow of death, I will fear no evil: for Thou art with me; Thy rod and Thy staff | they — | comfort me.

3 Thou preparest a table before me in the presence of mine enemies: Thou anointest my head with oil: my | cup . . runneth | over. ‖ Surely goodness and mercy shall follow me all the days of my life; and I will dwell in the house of the | Lord, for | ever. ‖ A- | men.

GOD BLESS OUR SCHOOL.

ALFRED TAYLOR.

With vigor.

1. God bless our school! Sing to the praise of God most high; Sing how He sent His
2. God bless our school! Bring all the wand'ring children in, Bring all the heirs of

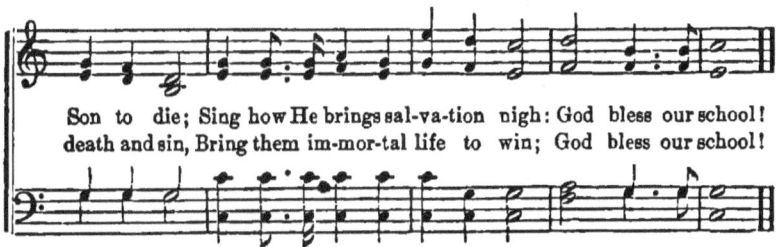

Son to die; Sing how He brings sal-va-tion nigh: God bless our school!
death and sin, Bring them im-mor-tal life to win; God bless our school!

3. God bless our school!
Teach us the word of truth to know,
Teach us in Christian strength to grow,
Teach us to serve Thee here below!
God bless our school!

4. God bless our school!
Fill all our hearts with heavenly grace,
Lead us in love to that blest place
Where we shall see our Savior's face.
God bless our school!

HOLY, HOLY, HOLY! LORD GOD ALMIGHTY.

J. B. Dykes.

1. Ho - ly, Ho - ly, Ho - ly! Lord God Al - might - y!
2. Ho - ly, Ho - ly, Ho - ly! all the saints a - dore Thee;

Ear - ly in the morn-ing our song shall rise to Thee;
Cast - ing down their golden crowns around the glass - y sea;

Ho - ly, Ho - ly, Ho - ly! mer - ci - ful and might - y;
Cher - u - bim and Ser - aphim fall-ing down be - fore Thee,

God in Three Per - sons, Bless - ed Trin - i - ty! Amen.
Which wert, and art, and ev - er more shalt be.

3 Holy, Holy, Holy! though the darkness hide Thee,
    Though the eye of sinful man Thy glory may not see,
  Only Thou art Holy: There is none beside Thee
    Perfect in power, in love, and purity.

4 Holy, Holy, Holy! Lord God Almighty!
    All Thy works shall praise Thy Name, in earth, and sky, and sea:
  Holy, Holy, Holy! merciful and mighty;
    God in Three Persons, Blessed Trinity! Amen.

R. Heber.

R. BROWN BORTHWICK.

1. Al - le - lu - ia! Fair - est morn - ing! Fair - er
2. Sun - day, full of ho - ly glo - ry! Sweet - est

than our words can say! Down we lay the heav - y bur - den
rest - day of the soul! Light up - on a world of dark - ness

Of life's toil and care to - day; While this morn of joy and
From thy bless - ed moments roll! Ho - ly, hap - py, heav'nly

love Brings fresh vig - or from a - bove.
day, Thou canst charm our grief a - way. A - men.

3. In the gladness of His worship
   We will seek our joy to-day:
   It is then we learn the fullness
   Of the grace for which we pray,
   When the word of life is given,
   Like the Savior's voice from heaven.

4 Let the day with Thee be ended,
   As with Thee it has begun;
   And Thy blessing, Lord, be granted,
   Till earth's days and weeks are done;
   That at last Thy servants may
   Keep eternal Sabbath-day. Amen.

BLUMENTHAL.

1. Now the shades of night are gone; Now the morning light is come;

Lord, may we be thine to - day; Drive the shades of sin a - way.

2. Fill our souls with heav'nly light; Ban - ish doubt and clear our sight;

In thy serv-ice, Lord, to - day, May we la - bor, watch and pray.

3 Keep our wayward passions bound;
Save us from our foes around;
Going out and coming in,
Keep us safe from every sin.

4 When our work of life is past,
Oh, receive us then at last;
Night and sin will be no more
When we reach the heavenly shore.

S. B. GOULD. J. BARNBY.

1. Now the day is o - ver, Night is draw-ing nigh,

Shad - ows of the eve - ning Steal a - cross the sky.

2 Jesus, give the weary
Calm and sweet repose;
With Thy tenderest blessing
May our eyelids close.

3 Grant to little children
Visions bright of Thee;
Guard the sailors tossing
On the deep blue sea.

4 Through the long night-watches,
May Thine angels spread
Their white wings above me,
Watching round my bed.

5 When the morning wakens,
Then may I arise,
Pure and fresh and sinless
In Thy holy eyes.

ALL FOR GOD.

F. R. HAVERGAL. C. S. H.

1. Take my life and let it be Con - se - crat - ed, Lord, to Thee;

Take my hands, and let them move At the im - pulse of Thy love.

2 Take my feet, and let them be
Swift and beautiful for Thee;
Take my voice, and let me sing
Always only for my King.

3 Take my silver and my gold—
Not a mite would I withhold;
Take my moments and my days—
Let them flow in ceaseless praise.

4 Take my will and make it Thine—
It shall be no longer mine;
Take my heart, it is thine own:
It shall be Thy royal throne.

5 Take my love; my Lord, I pour
At Thy feet its treasure-store;
Take myself, and I will be
Ever, only, all for Thee.

SUN OF MY SOUL, THOU SAVIOR DEAR.

JOHN KEBLE.   ARR. W. H. MONK.

1. Sun of my soul, thou Sav - ior dear, It is not

night if Thou be near: Oh, may no earth - born

cloud a - rise To hide Thee from Thy serv - ant's eyes.

"Abide with us." Luke 24: 29.

2 When the soft dews of kindly sleep
My wearied eyelids gently steep,
Be my last thought, how sweet to rest
Forever on my Savior's breast.

3 Abide with me from morn till eve,
For without Thee I can not live;
Abide with me when night is nigh,
For without Thee I dare not die.

4 If some poor wandering child of Thine
Have spurned, to-day, the voice divine,
Now, Lord, the gracious work begin;
Let him no more lie down in sin.

5 Watch by the sick; enrich the poor
With blessings from Thy boundless store:
Be every mourner's sleep to-night,
Like infant's slumbers, pure and light.

6 Come near and bless us when we wake,
Ere through the world our way we take;
Till, in the ocean of Thy love,
We lose ourselves in heaven above.

1 New every morning is the love
Our wakening and uprising prove;
Through sleep and darkness safely brought,
Restored to life, and power, and thought.

2 New mercies, each returning day,
Hover around us while we pray;
New perils past, new sins forgiven,
New thoughts of God, new hopes of heaven.

3 If on our daily course our mind
Be set to hallow all we find,
New treasures still of countless price
God will provide for sacrifice.

4 The trivial round, the common task,
Will furnish all we ought to ask:
Room to deny ourselves; a road
To bring us daily nearer God.

5 Only, O Lord, in Thy dear love
Fit us for perfect rest above;
And help us, this and every day,
To live more nearly as we pray.

JOHN KEBLE.

A. H. BROWN.

1. The day is past and o - ver; All thanks, O Lord! to Thee;

We pray thee now that sin - less The hours of dark may be;

O Je - sus! keep us in thy sight, And guard us thro' the coming night.

2 The day is past and over;
  We raise our hymn to thee;
And ask that free from peril
  The hours of dark may be;
O Jesus! keep us in thy sight,
And guard us through the coming night.

3 Be thou our souls' preserver,
  O God! for thou dost know
How many are the perils
  Through which we have to go;
O loving Jesus! hear our call,
And guard and save us from them all.

PRAISE GOD FROM WHOM ALL BLESSINGS FLOW.

L. M.

1. Praise God, from whom all blessings flow; Praise Him, all creatures here below.

Praise Him a-bove, ye heavenly host; Praise Father, Son, and Ho-ly Ghost.

"WE MARCH, WE MARCH TO VICTORY."

J. BARNBY.

We march, we march to vic - to - ry, With the Cross of the Lord be -

fore us, With His lov - ing eye look-ing down from the sky, And His

Ho - ly Arm spread o'er us, His Ho - ly Arm spread o'er us. 1. We

His Arm

come in the might of the Lord of Light, In gladsome train to meet Him;
tread to the roll of the or - gan swell, With the watchword duly giv - en;

And we put to flight the arm-ies of night, That the sons of the day may
And we challenge the Prince of the Hosts of Hell To fight for the Gates of

greet Him, The sons of the day may greet Him. We march, we march to
Heav - en: To fight for the Gates of Heav - en. We march, etc.

vic - to - ry, With the Cross of the Lord be - fore us, With His

lov - ing eye look-ing down from the sky, And His Holy Arm spread o'er us.

| All verses except last. | Last verse only. |

(2d verse.)

His Ho - ly Arm spread o'er us. We o'er us. A - men.

His Arm

3 And the choir of Angels with songs
    awaits
Our march to the golden Sion;
For our Captain has broken the bra-
    zen gates
And burst the bars of iron:
    We march, we march, etc.

4 Then onward we march, our arms to
    prove,
With the banner of Christ before us,
With His eye of love looking down
    from above,
And His Holy Arm spread o'er us.
    We march, we march, etc.

ONWARD, CHRISTIAN SOLDIERS.

S. BARING GOULD.　　　　　　　　　　　　　　　A. S. SULLIVAN.

1. Onward, Christian Soldiers, Marching as to war, With the cross of Jesus Going on be-fore. Christ, the royal Mas-ter, Leads against the foe; Forward in-to bat-tle, See, his banners go! Onward, Christian soldiers, Marching as to war, With the cross of Jesus Go-ing on be-fore.

2 At the sign of triumph
　Satan's host doth flee;
On then, Christian soldiers,
　On to victory.
Hell's foundations quiver
　At the shout of praise;
Brothers, lift your voices,
　Loud your anthems raise.

3 Like a mighty army
　Moves the Church of God;
Brothers, we are treading
　Where the saints have trod;
We are not divided,
　All one body we,
One in hope and doctrine,
　One in charity.

4 Crowns and thrones may perish,
　Kingdoms rise and wane,
But the Church of Jesus
　Constant will remain;
Gates of hell can never
　'Gainst that Church prevail;
We have Christ's own promise,
　And that can not fail.

5 Onward, then, ye people,
　Join our happy throng,
Blend with ours your voices
　In the triumph-song;
Glory, laud, and honor
　Unto Christ, the King,
This through countless ages
　Men and angels sing.

T. J. POTTER.   HAYDN.

1. Brightly gleams our banner, Pointing to the sky, Waving wand'rers onward
2. Jesus, Lord and Mas-ter, At Thy sa-cred feet, Here with hearts rejoicing

To their home on high. Journeying o'er the desert, Gladly thus we pray,
See Thy children meet: Often have we left Thee, Often gone a - stray,

And with hearts unit - ed Take our heavenward way. Brightly gleams our banner,
Keep us, mighty Savior, In the narrow way. Brightly gleams, etc.

Pointing to the sky, Waving wand'rers onward To their home on high. A - men.

3 All our days direct us
  In the way we go,
  Lead us on victorious
  Over every foe;
  Bid Thine angels shield us
  When the storm-clouds lour,
  Pardon Thou and save us
  In the last dread hour.
    Brightly gleams, etc.

4 Then with saints and angels
  May we join above,
  Offering prayers and praises
  At Thy throne of love;
  When the toil is over,
  Then comes rest and peace,
  Jesus, in his beauty,
  Songs that never cease.
    Brightly gleams, etc.

2

ABIDE WITH ME.

H. F. LYTE.

W. H. MONK.

1. A - bide with me; fast falls the ev - en - tide; The darkness

deep - ens; Lord, with me a - bide; When oth - er help - ers

fail, and comforts flee, Help of the helpless, oh, a - bide with me.

2 Swift to its close ebbs out life's little day;
Earth's joys grow dim, its glories pass away;
Change and decay in all around I see;
O Thou, who changest not, abide with me.

3 I need Thy presence every passing hour;
What but Thy grace can foil the tempter's power?
Who like Thyself my guide and stay can be
Thro' cloud and sunshine, oh, abide with me.

4 I fear no foe, with Thee at hand to bless;
Ills have no weight, and tears no bitterness;
Where is death's sting? where, grave, thy victory?
I triumph still, if Thou abide with me.

5 Hold Thou Thy cross before my closing eyes,
Shine thro' the gloom and point me to the skies,
Heaven's morning breaks, and earth's vain shadows flee;
In life, in death, O Lord, abide with me.

MY GOD, MY FATHER, WHILE I STRAY.

CHARLOTTE ELLIOT.

A. H. D. TROYTE.

1. My God, my Father while I stray, Far from my home on life's rough way,

Oh, teach me from my heart to say, "Thy will be done." A - men.

2 What though in lonely grief I sigh,
For friends b loved no longer nigh,
Submissive still would I reply,
"Thy will be done."

3 If Thou shouldst call me to resign
What most I prize—it ne'er was mine;
I only yield Thee what was Thine:—
"Thy will be done."

4 Renew my will from day to day,
Blend it with Thine, and take away
All that now makes it hard to say,
"Thy will be done."

5 If but my fainting heart be blest
With Thy sweet Spirit for its guest,
My God, to Thee I leave the rest;
"Thy will be done."

COME, MY SOUL, THOU MUST BE WAKING.

F. R. Louis.   J. Stainer.

1. Come, my soul, thou must be waking; Now is breaking O'er the earth a-
noth - er day; Come, to Him who made this splen-dor,
See thou ren - der All thy fee - ble strength can pay. A - men.

2 Gladly hail the light returning;
Ready burning
Be the incense of thy powers;
For the night is safely ended;
God hath tended
With His care thy helpless hours.

3 Pray that He may prosper ever
Each endeavor,
When thine aim is good and true;
But that He may ever thwart thee,
And convert thee,
When thou evil wouldst pursue.

4 Think that He thy ways beholdeth,
He unfoldeth
Every fault that lurks within,
He the hidden shame glossed over·
Can discover,
And discern each deed of sin.

5 Mayest thou on life's last morrow,
Free from sorrow,
Pass away in slumber sweet;
And, released from death's dark sadness,
Rise in gladness
That far brighter Sun to greet.

6 Only God's free gifts abuse not,
Light refuse not,
But His Spirit's voice obey;
Thou with Him shalt dwell, beholding
Light unfolding
All things in unclouded day.

7 Glory, honor, exaltation,
Adoration,
Be to the Eternal One:
To the Father, Son, and Spirit,
Praise and merit,
While unending ages run. Amen.

GOLDEN HARPS ARE SOUNDING.

FRANCES R. HAVERGAL.

PERRINA.

1. Gold - en harps are sound - ing, An - gel voi - ces ring;
D.C. All His work is end - ed, Joy - ful - ly we sing;

Pear - ly gates are o - pened, O - pened for the King.
Je - sus hath as - cend - ed, Glo - ry to our King.

Christ the King of glo - ry, Je - sus King of love,

Is gone up in tri - umph To His throne a - bove.

2 He who came to save us,
 He who bled below,
 Now is crowned with gladness
 At His Father's side.
 Never more to suffer,
 Never more to die,
 Jesus King of glory
 Is gone up on high.
 All His work, etc.

3 Praying for His children
 In that blessed place,
 Calling them to glory,
 Sending them His grace;
 His bright home preparing,
 Little ones, for you;
 Jesus ever liveth,
 Ever loveth too.
 All His work, etc.

G. THRING.   ARR. by JOS. P. HOLBROOK.

1. Savior, bless - ed Sav - ior, Listen whilst we sing, Hearts and voices
2. Near-er, ev - er near - er, Christ, we draw to Thee, Deep in ad - o-

rais - ing,   Praises to   our King.   All we have to of - fer;
ra - tion   Bending low the knee: Thou for our   redemption

All we hope to be,   Bod-y, soul, and spir-it, All we yield to
Cam'st on earth to die; Thou, that we might follow, Hast gone up on

Thee,   Bod - y, soul, and spirit,   All we yield to Thee.
high,   Thou, that we might follow,   Hast gone up on high.

3 Onward, ever onward,
   Journeying o'er the road
Worn by saints before us,
   Journeying on to God:
Leaving all behind us,
   May we hasten on,
Backward never looking,
   Till the prize is won.

4 Brighter still and brighter
   Glows the western sun,
Shedding all its gladness
   O'er our work that's done;
Time will soon be over,
   Toil and sorrow past,
May we, blessed Savior,
   Find a rest at last.

Thomas Kelly.   German Melody.

1. Sing of Je - sus, sing for - ev - er,   Of the love that changes nev - er.

Who or what from Him can sev - er   Those He makes His   own?

Ps. xxvi. 2.

2 With His blood the Lord has bought
    them ;
   When they knew Him not, He sought
    them,
   And from all their wanderings brought
    them;
     His the praise alone.

3 Through the desert Jesus leads them,
   With the bread of heaven He feeds them,
   And through all the way He speeds them
     To their home above.

4 There they see the Lord who bought
    them,
   Him who came from heaven, and sought
    them,
   Him who by His Spirit taught them,
     Him they serve and love.

1 Saints in glory, we together
   Know the song that ceases never;
   Song of songs Thou art, O Savior,
     All that endless day.

2 Come, ye angels, round us gather,
   While to Jesus we draw nearer;
   In His throne He'll seat forever
     Those for whom He died.

3 Underneath His throne a river,
   Clear as crystal, flows forever,
   Like His fullness, failing never:
     Hail, enthronéd Lamb!

4 O the unsearchable Redeemer!
   Shoreless Ocean, sounded never!
   Yesterday, to-day, forever,
     Jesus Christ, the same.

S. E. Mahmied.

J. H. GILLMORE. Arr. by J. P. HOLBROOK.

1. He lead-eth me! O bless-ed thought, O words with heavenly
2. Sometimes 'mid scenes of deep-est gloom, Sometimes where E-den's
3. Lord, I would clasp Thy hand in mine, Nor ev-er mur-mur
4. And when my task on earth is done, When, by Thy grace, the

comfort fraught, Whate'er I do, where-e'er I be, Still 'tis God's
bow-ers bloom, By wa-ters still, o'er troubled sea—Still 'tis His
nor re-pine—Con-tent whatev-er lot I see, Since 'tis my
victory's won, E'en death's cold wave I will not flee, Since God thro'

CHORUS.

hand that lead-eth me!
hand that lead-eth me! He lead-eth me! He lead-eth me! By
God that lead-eth me!
Jor-dan lead-eth me!

His own hand He lead-eth me; He leadeth me! He leadeth me!

COME, CHILDREN, JOIN AND SING.

ROSSINI.

1. Come, children, join and sing, Loud praise to Christ, our King; Let all with
GIRLS. 2. Come, lift your hearts on high, Let praises fill the sky, He is our
3. Praise we the Lord a-gain, Life shall not end the strain: On heaven's

heart and voice, Be-fore His throne re-joice. Praise Christ, our King!
guide and friend, His love shall nev-er end. Praise Christ, our King!
bliss-ful shore, His goodness we'll a-dore. Praise Christ, our King!

SOLO.

Organ. Organ. **FULL CHORUS.**

Praise Christ, our King! Come, children, join and sing, Loud praise to
Praise Christ, our King! Come, lift your hearts on high, Let praises
Praise Christ, onr King! Praise we the Lord again, Life shall not

Christ, our King! Let all with heart and voice, Before His throne rejoice.
fill the sky, He is our guide and friend, His love shall never end.
end the strain: On heaven's blissful shore, His goodness we'll adore.

Miss E. CAMPBELL.   Arr. J. P. HOLBROOK.

1. {
What means this ea - ger anx - ious throng,   Pressing the
These wond-rous gather-ings day   by   day?   This strange com-
}

{
Who is   this Je - sus? Why should He The cit - y
Ev'n chil - dren hear   His gra - cious word, And hail   Him
}

bu - sy streets a - long? }
mo - tion by the way? } The voic - es of the throng re-
move so might - i - ly? }
Da - vid's Son and Lord. } Ho-san - nas min - gle with the

ply:— "Je - sus of Naz - a - reth pass - eth by!"
cry,   "Je - sus of Naz - a - reth pass - eth by!"

3 Jesus! 'tis He who once below
Man's pathway trod in pain and woe;
And burdened ones, where'er He came,
Brought out their sick, and deaf, aud
    lame;
Blind men rejoiced to hear the cry,
"Jesus of Nazareth passeth by!"

4 Again He comes; from place to place
His holy footprints we can trace.
Ho! all ye heavy-laden, come!
Here's pardon, comfort, rest, a home.
Lost wanderers here's a refuge nigh;
Jesus of Nazareth passeth by!

1. All is bright and cheerful round us, All a - bove is soft and blue;

Spring at last hath come and found us, Spring and all its pleasures too;

Ev-'ry flower is full of glad-ness, Dew is bright and birds are gay;

Earth, with all its sin and sadness, Seems a happy place to-day. A-men.

2 If the flowers, that fade so quickly,
  If a day, that ends in night,
If the sky, that clouds so thickly
  Often cover from our sight,—
If they all have so much beauty,
  What must be God's Land of Rest,
Where His sons, that do their duty,
After many toils are blest ?

3 There are leaves that never wither,
  There are flowers that ne'er decay;
Nothing evil goeth thither,
  Nothing good is kept away.
They that came from tribulation,
  Washed their robes and made them white,
Out of every tongue and nation,
  They have rest, and peace, and light.
                            Amen.

WE ARE WATCHING, WE ARE WAITING. 27

GEO. F. ROOT.
By per. of John Church & Co.

Slow.

1. We are watching, we are wait-ing, For the bright prophet - ic day;
2. We are watching, we are wait-ing, For the star that brings the day;
3. We are watching, we are wait-ing, For the beauteous King of day;

When the shadows, wea - ry shadows, From the world shall roll a - way.
When the night of sin shall vanish, And the shadows melt a - way.
For the Chiefest of ten thousand, For the Light, the Truth, the Way.

CHORUS.

We are wait-ing for the morning, When the beauteous day is dawning,

We are wait-ing for the morning, For the gold-en spires of day.

Lo! He comes! see the King draw near; Zion shout the Lord is here.

"Songs of Love." H. R. PALMER.

1. An - gry words! oh, let them nev - er From the tongue un - bri - dled
2. Love is much too pure and ho - ly; Friendship is too sa - cred
3. An - gry words are light - ly spoken; Bitterest tho'ts are rash - ly

slip; May the heart's best impulse ev - er Check them e'er they soil the lip.
far, For a moment's reck-less fol - ly Thus to des - o - late and mar.
stirred; Brightest links of life are bro-ken By a sin-gle an-gry word.

CHORUS.

Love one an-oth - er, Thus saith the Savior, Children obey thy Father's blest com-

Love each other, Love each other, 'Tis thy Father's blest com-

mand; Love one another, Thus saith the Savior, Children obey His blest command.

mand; Love each other, Love each other, 'Tis His blest command.

S. S. Hymnal.

1. What though be-fore me it is dark, Too dark for me to see?
2. It may be that my path is rough, Thorny, and hard, and steep;
3. Per - haps my path is ver - y short, My jour - ney near - ly done;

I ask but light for one step more, 'Tis quite e-nough for me.
And, knowing this, my strength might fail, Thro' fear and ter - ror deep.
And I might trem-ble at the thought Of end - ing it so soon.

I would not see my fur-ther path, 'Tis mer - cy vails it so;
It may be that it winds a - long A smooth and flow - 'ry way;
And so I do not wish to see My jour-ney thro' its length;

My pres - ent steps might hard-er be, Did I the fu - ture know.
But see - ing this, I might de-spise The jour-ney of to - day.
As - sured that thro' my Fa-ther's love, Each step will find its strength.

Unknown.

1. Fair - est Lord Je - sus! Rul - er of all na - ture!
2. Fair are the mead-ows, Fair - er still the wood-lands,
3. Fair is the sun - shine, Fair - er still the moonlight,

Oh, Thou of God and man the Son! Thee will I cher-ish,
Robed in the bloom - ing garb of spring; Je - sus is fair - er,
And the twink - ling star - ry host; Je - sus shines brighter,

Thee will I hon - or, Thou, my soul's glo-ry, joy, and crown.
Je - sus is pur - er, Who makes the woe-ful heart to sing.
Je - sus shines pur - er, Than all the an-gels heaven can boast.

GOD, MY KING, THY MIGHT.

R. MANT.   I. CONKEY.

1. God, my King, Thy might confessing, Ev - er will I bless Thy name;
2. All Thy works, O Lord! shall bless Thee, Thee shall all Thy saints adore;

Day by day Thy throne addressing, Still will I Thy praise proclaim.
King supreme shall they confess Thee And proclaim Thy sovereign power.

J. M. NEALE, Tr. Arr. J. P. HOLBROOK.

1. Those e-ter-nal bow-ers Man hath nev-er trod, Those unfad-ing
2. He who glad-ly bar-ters All on earth-ly ground; He who, like the
3. While I do my du-ty, Struggling thro' the tide, Whisper thou of

flow-ers, Round the throne of God; Who may hope to gain them
mar-tyrs, Says, "I will be crowned;" He whose one ob-la-tion
beau-ty On the oth-er side. Soon for-got the sto-ry

Aft-er wea-ry fight? Who at length attain them Clad in robes of white?
Is a life of love; Clinging to the na-tion Of the blest a-bove.
Of our brief dis-tress; Oh, the fu-ture glo-ry! Oh, the love-li-ness!

GOD'S FREE MERCY STREAMETH.

1 God's free mercy streameth
Over all the world,
And His banner gleameth
Every where unfurled,
Broad and deep and glorious
As the heavens above,
Shines in might victorious
His eternal love.

2 Lord, upon our blindness
Thy pure radiance pour;
For Thy loving kindness
Make us love Thee more.

And when clouds are drifting
Dark across our sky,
Then, the veil uplifting,
Father, be Thou nigh.

3 We will never doubt Thee
Though Thou veil Thy light;
Life is dark without Thee,
Death with Thee is bright.
Light of light! shine o'er us,
On our pilgrim way;
Go Thou still before us
To the endless day.

H. P. SMITH.

COME UNTO ME, YE WEARY.

W. C. Dix.　　　　　　　　　　　　　　　　J. P. Holbrook, by per.

1. "Come un - to me, ye wea - ry, And I will give you rest."
2. "Come un - to me, ye wanderers, And I will give you light."

O blessed voice of Je - sus, Which comes to hearts oppressed!
O lov-ing voice of Je - sus, Which comes to cheer the night!

It tells of ben - e - dic - tion, Of par - don, grace and peace
Our hearts were filled with sad - ness, And we had lost our way,

Of joy that hath no end - ing, Of love that can - not cease.
But He has brought us glad - ness, And songs at break of day.

3 "Come unto me, ye fainting,
　　And I will give you life.
O cheering voice of Jesus,
　　Which comes to aid our strife!
The foe is stern and eager,
　　The fight is fierce and long;
But thou hast made us mighty,
　　And stronger than the strong.

4 "And whosoever cometh,
　　I will not cast him out."
O welcome voice of Jesus,
　　Which drives away our doubt,
Which calls us, very sinners,
　　Unworthy though we be
Of love so free and boundless,
　　To come, dear Lord, to Thee!

Copyright, 1881, by J. P. Holbrook.

Arr. J. P. Holbrook, by per.

1. Mansions are prepared a-bove, By the gracious God of love;
2. Crowns that daz-zle hu - man eye, Wait for those who reach the sky;

Cres.

Ma-ny will those mansions see— Is there one pre-pared for me?
Ma-ny there, those crowns will see, Is there one pre-pared for me?

CHORUS.

Is there one pre-pared for me? Is there one for me?

Ma-ny will those mansions see, Is there one prepared for me?

3 Robes of spotless white are given,
By the glorious King of heaven;
All can have them, they are free,—
Is there one prepared for me?

4 Harps of joyful sound above,
Swell the praise of Jesus' love;
Oh! how sweet their strains will be,
Is there, Lord, a harp for me?

3

ANGEL VOICES EVER SINGING.

F. POTT.
A. SULLIVAN.

1. Angel voices ever singing Round Thy throne of light, Angel harps forever ringing,
2. Thou, who art beyond the farthest Mental eye can scan, Can it be that Thou regardest

Rest not day nor night; Thousands only live to bless Thee, And confess Thee Lord of might.
Songs of sinful man? Can we feel that Thou art near us, And wilt hear us? Yea, we can.

3 Yea, we know Thy love rejoices
　　O'er each work of Thine!
　Thou didst ears and hands and voices
　　For Thy praise combine!
　Craftsman's art and music's measure
　　For Thy pleasure, didst design.

4 Here, great God, to-day we offer
　　Of Thine own to Thee;
　And for Thine acceptance proffer,
　　All unworthily,
　Hearts and minds, and hands and voices,
　　In our choicest melody.
　　　　　　　　Amen.

AS CHRIST UPON THE CROSS.

E. CASWALL.
H. SMART.

1. As Christ up-on the cross His head in-clined,
2. So now her-self my soul Would whol-ly give,

And to His Father's hands His part-ing soul re-signed.
In-to His sa-cred charge, In whom all spir-its live.

3 Thus would I live; yet now
　　Not I, but He
　In all His power and love
　　Henceforth alive in me.

4 One Sacred Trinity!
　　One Lord Divine!
　May I be ever His,
　　And He forever mine.

ANON.　　　　　　　　　　J. P. HOLBROOK. BY per.

1. Pur-er yet and pur-er I would be in mind, Dear-er yet and

dear - er Ev - 'ry du - ty find; Hop - ing still and trust - ing

God without a fear, Patient-ly be - liev - ing He will make all clear.

1 Purer yet and purer
  I would be in mind,
Dearer yet and dearer
  Every duty find;
Hoping still and trusting
God without a fear,
Patiently believing
  He will make all clear.

2 Calmer yet and calmer
  Trial bear and pain,
Surer yet and surer
  Peace at last to gain;
Suffering still and doing,
To His will resigned,
And to God subduing
  Heart and will and mind.

3 Higher yet and higher
  Out of clouds and night,
Nearer yet and nearer
  Rising to the light—
Light serene and holy,
  Where my soul may rest,
Purified and lowly,
  Sanctified and blest.

1 Brighter still and brighter
  Glows the western sun,
Shedding all its gladness
  O'er our work that's done;
Time will soon be over,
  Toil and sorrow past,
May we, blessed Savior,
  Find a rest at last!

2 Onward, ever onward,
  Journeying o'er the road
Worn by saints before us,
  Journeying on to God;
Leaving all behind us,
  May we hasten on,
Backward never looking
  Till the prize is won.

3 Higher then, and higher,
  Bear the ransomed soul,
Earthly toils forgotten,
  Savior, to its goal;
Where, in joys unthought of,
  Saints with angels sing,
Never weary, raising
  Praises to their King.
　　　　　　　　　G. THRING.

MY AIN COUNTRIE.

Miss M. A. LEE.

Scotch Song.

1. { I am far frae my hame, an' I'm wea-ry af-tenwhiles, For the
I'll ... ne'er be fu' con-tent, un-til my een do see The

D. C. But these sichts an' these soun's will as naething be to me, When I

| 1st time. | 2d time. Fine. |

lang'd-for hame-bringing, an' my Father's welcome smiles; }
gow-den gates of heav'n, an' my (*Omit.*) . . . . . . } ain coun-trie.
hear the an-gels singing in my (*Omit.*) . . . . . . ain coun-trie.

D. C.

{ The earth is fleck'd wi' flow-ers, mon-y-tint-ed, fresh, and gay; }
{ The bird-ies war-ble blithe-ly, for my Fa-ther made them sae; }

2 I've His gude word of promise that some gladsome day the King,
To His ain royal palace, His banished hame will bring
Wi' een, an' wi' heart running owre we shall see
"The King in His beauty," an' our ain countrie.
My sins hae been mony, and my sorrows hae been sair;
But there they'll never vex me, nor be remembered mair;
For His bluid hath made me white, and His hand shall dry my e'e,
When He brings me hame at last to my ain countrie.

2 Like a bairn to its mither, a wee birdie to its nest,
I wad fain be ganging noo unto my Savior's breast,
For He gathers in His bosom witless worthless lambs like me,
An' "He carries them Himsel'," to His ain countrie.
He's faithfu' that hath promised, He'll surely come again,
He'll keep His tryst wi' me, at what hour I dinna ken;
But He bids me still to wait, an' ready aye to be,
To gang at ony moment to my ain countrie.

3 So I'm watching aye, and singing o' my hame as I wait,
For the soun'ing o' His footfa' this side the gowden gate,
God gie His grace to ilk ane wha listens noo to me,
That we may a' gang in gladness to our ain countrie.

[*Last four lines of 1st verse can be sung to complete 4th verse.*]

WM. MITCHELL.   JOHN J. HOOD.

1. It's a bon-nie, bon-nie worl' that we're liv-in' in the noo, An'
sun-ny is the lan' we aft-en traivel throo; But in vain we look for
something to which oor' hearts can cling, For its beauty is as naething to the
snowflakes, an' the down on winter's wing, It's fine to ken it daurna touch the
Pal-ace o' the King. We like the gilded simmer, wi' its mer-ry, mer-ry
tread, An' we sigh when hoary winter lays its beauties wi' the dead;

D. S. For tho' bonnie are the

2 Then, again, I've juist been thinkin' that when a' thing here's sae bricht,
The sun in a' its grandeur, an' the mune wi' quiv'rin' licht,
The ocean in the simmer, or the woodland in the spring,
What maun it be up yonner, in the Palace o' the King!
It's here we hae oor trials, an' it's here that He prepares
A' His chosen for the raiment which the ransomed sinner wears,
An' it's here that He wad hear us 'mid oor tribulations sing, —
"We'll trust oor God, wha reigneth in the Palace o' the King.

GLAD AND FREE.

Rev. A. A. Hoskin.   J. M. Stillman.

1. Glad and free, glad and free, Je - sus, we will fol - low thee;
2. Glad and free, glad and free, Je - sus, we will work for thee;
3. Glad and free, glad and free, Je - sus, we will sing to thee;
4. Glad and free, glad and free, Je - sus, we will live for thee;

Glad - ly free from all a-larms, Safe - ly shield - ed from all harms;
Glad - ly work with all our might,Conqu'ring wrong and do - ing right;
Glad - ly sing - ing songs of praise, For the love which crowns our days;
All our lives we glad - ly give, Un - to Him who lets us live;

We will follow ev-'ry day In Thy safe and narrow way; Glad and free,
Working for Thee ev-'ry day,Trusting in Thy strength alway; Glad and free,
Glad - ly sing-ing ev-'ry day, All a - long life's happy way; Glad and free,
And in heav'n thou wilt repay, All who live for thee each day; Glad and free,

glad and free, Je - sus, we will fol - low Thee, we will fol - low Thee.
glad and free, Je - sus, we will work for Thee, we will work for Thee.
glad and free, Je - sus, we will sing to Thee, we will sing to Thee.
glad and free, Je - sus, we will live for Thee, we will live for Thee.

From "Good Will" by per. Towne & Stillman.

JOHN BOWRING.

*

1. God is love; His mer - cy bright - ens All the path in
3. E'en the hour that dark - est seem - eth Will His change - less

which we rove; Bliss He wakes, And woe He light - ens:
D. S. But His mer - cy wan - eth nev - er:
good - ness prove; From the mist His bright - ness stream - eth:
D. S. Ev - 'ry - where His glo - ry shin - eth:

Fine.

God is wis - dom, God is love. 2. Chance and change are
God is wis - dom, God is love.
God is wis - dom, God is love. 4. He with earth - ly
God is wis - dom, God is love.

D. S.

bus - y ev - er; Man de - cays, and a - ges move;
cares en - twin - eth Hope and com - fort from a - bove:

THE BETTER LAND.

Rev. E. P. PARKER.
From S. S. Hymnal, by per.

1. Whither, pil - grims, are you go - ing, Each with staff in hand?

"We are go - ing on a jour - ney, At the King's command.

O - ver plains and hills aud val - leys, We are

go - ing to His pal - ace, In the bet - ter land."

2 Tell me, pilgrims, what you hope for
  In the better land?
ˣSpotless robes and crowns of glory,
  From the Savior's hand.
We shall drink of life's clear river,
We shall dwell with God forever
  In the better land."

3 Will you let me travel with you
  To the better land?
"Come away, we bid you welcome
  To our little band.
Come, oh, come, we can not leave you,
Christ is waiting to receive you
  In the better land."

H. BONAR.   J. P. HOLBROOK. By per.

1. What a friend we have in Je-sus, All our sins and griefs to bear;

What a priv-i-lege to car-ry Ev-'ry-thing to God in prayer.
D.S. All be-cause we do not car-ry Ev-'ry-thing to God in prayer.

Oh, what peace we oft-en for-feit, Oh, what needless pain we bear—

What a friend we have in Jesus,
  All our sins and griefs to bear;
What a privilege to carry
  Every thing to God in prayer.
Oh, what peace we often forfeit,
  Oh, what needless pain we bear—
All because we do not carry
  Every thing to God in prayer.

2 Have we trials and temptations?
  Is there trouble anywhere?
We should never be discouraged,
  Take it to the Lord in prayer.
Can we find a friend so faithful,
  Who will all our sorrows share?
Jesus knows our very weakness,
  Take it to the Lord in prayer.

1 One there is above all others,
  Well deserves the name of Friend,
His is love beyond a brother's,
  Costly, free, and knows no end.

2 Which of all our friends, to save us,
  Could or would have shed his blood?
But our Jesus died to have us
  Reconciled in Him to God.

3 When he lived on earth abaséd,
  Friend of sinners was His name;
Now, above all glory raiséd,
  He rejoices in the same.

4 Oh, for grace, our hearts to soften!
  Teach us, Lord, at length to love;
We, alas! forget too often
  What a friend we have above.
                   J. NEWTON.

MRS. M. G. SAFFERY.   THALBERG.

1. There is a lit-tle lone-ly fold, Whose flock One Shepherd keeps,

Through summer's heat and winter's cold, With eye that nev-er sleeps.

By e-vil beast, or burn-ing sky, Or damp of midnight air,

Not one in all that flock shall die Be-neath that Shepherd's care.

2 For if, unheeding or beguiled,
   In danger's path they roam,
His pity follows through the wild,
   And guards them safely home.

O gentle Shepherd, still behold
   Thy helpless charge in me;
And take a wanderer to Thy fold,
   That trembling turns to Thee.

WHEN HIS SALVATION BRINGING. 43

Rev. Joshua King.   T. R. Matthews.

1. When, His sal - va - tion bring - ing, To Zi - on Je - sus came,

The children all stood sing - ing Ho - san - na to His name.

Nor did their zeal of - fend Him, But as He rode a - long,

He let them still at - tend Him, And smiled to hear their song. A-men.

The Children in the Temple.
Matt. xxi. 15, 16.

2 And since the Lord retaineth
   His love to children still,
Though now as King He reigneth
   On Zion's heavenly hill;
We'll flock around His banner,
   We'll bow before His throne,
And cry aloud, Hosanna
   To David's royal Son.

3 For should we fail proclaiming
   Our great Redeemer's praise,
The stones, our silence shaming,
   Would their hosannas raise.
But shall we only render
   The tribute of our words?
No; while our hearts are tender,
   They too shall be the Lord's.

Mighty to save.
Is. lxiii. 1.

1 He comes in blood-stained garments;
   Upon His brow a crown;
The gates of brass fly open,
   The iron bands drop down;
From off the fettered captive
   The chains of Satan fall,
While angels shout triumphant,
   That Christ is Lord of all.

2 O Christ, His love is mighty,
   Long-suffering is His grace;
And glorious is the splendor
   That beameth from His face.
Our hearts up-leap in gladness
   When we behold that love,
As we go singing onward
   To dwell with Him above.

Mrs. Charitie Lees Bancroft.

IN THE SILENT MIDNIGHT WATCHES.

A. CLEVELAND COXE.

GEORGE F. ROOT.
By per. John Church & Co.

1. In the si - lent midnight watches, List,—thy bo - som door!

How it knocketh, knocketh, knocketh, Knocketh ev - er - more!

Say not 'tis thy pulse is beat-ing; 'Tis thy heart of sin;

'Tis thy Sav - ior knocks, and cri - eth, Rise, and let me in.

2 Death comes down with reckless foot-
step,
To the hall and hut!
Think you death will stand a-knocking
Where the door is shut?
Jesus waiteth, waiteth, waiteth,
But thy door is fast!
Grieved, away thy Savior goeth,
Death breaks in at last.

3 Then 'tis thine to stand entreat-
ing
Christ to let thee in;
At the gate of heaven beating,
Wailing for thy sin.
Nay, alas! thou foolish virgin,
Hast thou then forgot?
Jesus waited long to know thee,
But He knows thee not.

DR. MARCH.   P. P. VAN ARSDALE.

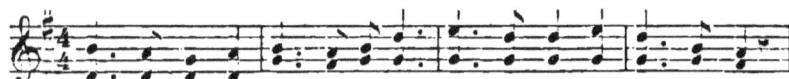

1. Hark! the voice of Je - sus calling, Who will go and work to - day;
2. If you can not cross the o-cean, And the heathen lands ex-plore,

Fields are white, the har-vest wait-ing, Who will bear the sheaves a - way?
You can find the heathen near-er, You can help them at your door;

Loud and long the Mas - ter call-eth, Rich re-ward He of - fers free;
If you can not give your thousands, You can give the wid-ow's mite,

Who will an-swer, glad - ly say-ing, "Here am I, O Lord, send me."
And the least you do for Je-sus, Will be precious in His sight.

If you can not speak like angels,
  If you can not preach like Paul,
You can tell the love of Jesus,
  You can say He died for all.
If you fail to rouse the wicked,
  With the judgment's dread alarms,
You may lead the little children
  To the Savior's waiting arms.

4 While the souls of men are dying,
  And the Master calls for you,
Let none hear you idly saying,
  "There is nothing I can do!"
Gladly take the task He gives you,
  Let His work your pleasure be,
Answer quickly when He calleth,
  Here am I, O Lord, send me."

IN THE KING'S ARMY.

EBEN E. REXFORD.   T. MARTIN TOWNE.

1. Behold, that blood-stain'd banner of the King! And hark! the rallying cry!
2. Behold, the allied hosts of wrong and sin, Drawn up in strong ar - ray!
3. En - list, en - list, the arm - y of the Lord Is gath-'ring for the fight;

"En - list, en - list, ex - ult-ing - ly it rings, Nor let Him pass you by."
Shut fast the gates, nor let them en-ter in! Christ holds the camp to-day!
And to the winds all doubts and fears they fling, Strong in their Leader's might.

CHORUS.

En-list! en-list! the mighty trumpets ring Earth's battle-fields a - cross,

Beneath the blood-stain'd banner of the King, A sol-dier of the cross.

4 Put on the armor of the King, I pray,
Oh, waiting, careless heart!
Christ or the world! he bids you choose to-day;
Oh, choose the better part!

5 Oh, blood-stain'd banner! he no more resists,
"Be Christ my King!" he cries;
Beneath Thy folds another heart enlists;
Oh, shout it to the skies!

From "Good Will," by permission of TOWNE & STILLMAN.

FANNY J. CROSBY.

S. J. VAIL.

1. Thou my ev - er - last-ing por-tion, More than friend or life to me,
2. Not for ease or worldly pleasure, Nor for fame my prayer shall be;
3. Lead me thro' the vale of shadows, Bear me o'er life's fit - ful sea;

All a - long my pilgrim journey, Sav-ior, let me walk with Thee.
Glad-ly will I toil and suf - fer, On - ly let me walk with Thee.
Then the gate of life e - ter - nal, May I en - ter, Lord, with Thee.

REFRAIN.

Close to Thee, close to Thee, Close to Thee, close to Thee;
Close to Thee, close to Thee, Close to Thee, close to Thee;
Close to Thee, close to Thee, Close to Thee, close to Thee;

All a - long my pilgrim jour-ney, Sav-ior, let me walk with Thee.
Glad-ly will I toil and suf - fer, On - ly let me walk with Thee.
Then the gate of life e - ter - nal, May I en - ter, Lord, with Thee.

WHITER THAN SNOW.

JAMES NICHOLSON.   WM. G. FISCHER.,

1. Dear Je - sus, I long to be per - fect - ly whole; I
2. Dear Je - sus, come down from Thy throne in the skies, And
3. Dear Je - sus, for this, I most hum - bly en - treat; I

want Thee for - ev - er to live in my soul; Break down every
help me to make a com-plete sac - ri - fice; I give up my-
wait, bless - ed Lord, sit-ting low at Thy feet, By faith, for my

i - dol, cast out ev - 'ry foe; Now wash me, and I shall be
self, and what-ev - er I know—Now wash me, and I shall be
cleansing, I see the blood flow—Now wash me, and I shall be

CHORUS.

whit - er than snow.
whit - er than snow. Whit - er than snow, yes, whit - er than
whit - er than snow.

snow; Now wash me, and I shall be whit - er than snow.

J. H. NEWMAN.

J. B. DYKES.

1. Lead, kindly Light, a-mid th'encircling gloom,   Lead Thou me
2. I   was not ev - er thus, nor prayed that Thou   Shouldst lead me
3. So long Thy power has blest me, sure it still   Will lead me

on; The night is dark, and I am far from home,   Lead Thou me
on; I loved to choose and see my path; but now   Lead Thou me
on; O'er moor and fen, o'er crag and torrent, till   The night is

on.   Keep Thou my   feet;   I   do   not   ask   to
on.   I   loved the   gar - ish day; and spite of
gone,   And with the   morn   those an - gel   fac - es

see   The dis - tant scene; one step e-nough   for   me.
fears,   Pride ruled my   will; remember not   past years.
smile,   Which I   have loved long since, and lost a - while.

4

WEARY OF EARTH, AND LADEN WITH MY SIN.

S. J. STONE.　　　　　　　　　　　　　　　　　J. LANGRAN.

1. Weary of earth, and laden with my sin, I look to heav'n, and long to enter in.

But there no evil thing may find a home, And yet I hear a voice that bids me "Come."

2 It is the voice of Jesus that I hear,
His are the hands stretched out to draw me near,
And His the blood that can for all atone,
And set me faultless there before the throne.

3 'Twas He who found me on the deathly wild,
And made me heir of heaven, the Father's child ;
And day by day, whereby my soul may live,
Gives me His grace of pardon, and will give.

4 Yea, Thou wilt answer for me, righteous Lord ;
Thine all the merits, mine the great reward;
Thine the sharp thorns, and mine the golden crown,
Mine the life won, and Thine the life laid down.

DEAR JESUS, EVER AT MY SIDE.

F. W. FABER.　　　　　　　　　　　　　　Arr. W. H. HAVERGAL.

1. Dear Je-sus, ev-er at my side, How lov-ing must Thou be,

To leave Thy home in heav'n to guard A lit-tle child like me.

2 I can not feel Thee touch my hand,
With pressure light and mild,
To check me as my mother did,
When I was but a child.

3 But I have felt thee in my thoughts,
Rebuking sin for me;
And, when my heart loves God, I know
The sweetness is from Thee.

4 And when, dear savior, I kneel down,
Morning and night, to prayer,
Something there is within my heart
Which tells me Thou art there.

5 Yes, when I pray, Thou prayest too;
Thy prayer is all for me;
But when I sleep, Thou sleepest not,
But watchest patiently.

GRACIOUS SAVIOR.

J. WHITTEMORE. J.

1. Gracious Sav - ior, gen - tle Shepherd, Lit - tle ones are dear to Thee;

Gathered with Thine arms, and carried In Thy bo - som may we be

Sweetly, fond-ly, safe-ly tend - ed, From all want and dan-ger free.

He shall feed His flock like a shepherd: He shall gather the lambs with His arm, and carry them in His bosom.—Isa. xl: 11.

2 Tender Shepherd, never leave us,
From Thy fold to go astray;
By Thy look of love directed,
May we walk the narrow way;
Thus direct us, and protect us,
Lest we fall an easy prey.

3 Cleanse our hearts from sinful folly
In the stream Thy love supplied,—
Mingled stream of Blood and Water
Flowing from Thy wounded side;
And to heavenly pastures lead us
Where Thine own still waters glide.

4 Let Thy holy word instruct us,
Keep our spirits pure and bright;
Let Thy love and grace constrain us
To approve whate'er is right,
Take Thine easy yoke, and wear it,
And to prove Thy burden light.

5 Taught to join the holy praises,
Which on earth Thy children sing,
Both with lips and hearts unfeigned,
May we our thank-offerings bring;
Then with all the saints in glory
Join to praise our Lord and King.

KINGSBURY.

1. Saw you nev - er in the twilight, When the sun has left the skies,

Up in heav'n the clear stars shining Thro' the gloom like sil-ver eyes?

So of old, the wise men, watching, Saw a lit - tle stranger star,

And they knew the King was giv-en, And they followed it from far.

2 Heard you never of the story
　How they crossed the desert wild,
Journeyed on by plain and mountain,
　Till they found the holy Child?
How they opened all their treasure,
　Kneeling to that infant King,
Gave the gold and fragrant incense,
　Gave the myrrh in offering?

3 Know you not that lowly infant
　Was the bright and Morning Star,
He who came to light the Gentiles
　And the darkened isles afar?
And we, too, may seek His cradle,
　There our hearts' best treasure bring,
Love and faith, and true devotion,
　For our Savior, God, and King.

2 Silent night! Holy night!
Shepherds quake at the sight;
Glories stream from heaven afar,
Heavenly hosts sing Alleluia!
Christ, the Savior, is born!
Christ, the Savior, is born!

3 Silent night! Holy night!
Son of God, love's pure light,
Radiant beams from Thy holy face
With the dawn of redeeming grace,
Jesus, Lord, at Thy birth!
Jesus, Lord, at Thy birth!

C. WESLEY.   MENDELSSOHN.

1. Hark, the her-ald an-gels sing, "Glo-ry to the new-born King!

Peace on earth, and mer-cy mild, God and sin-ners rec-on-ciled!"

Joy-ful, all ye na-tions, rise, Join the triumph of the skies;

U-ni-ver-sal nat-ure say, "Christ the Lord is born to-day,"

U-ni-ver-sal na-ture say, "Christ the Lord is born to-day."

2 Christ, by highest heaven adored,
Christ the everlasting Lord!
Late in time behold Him come,
Offspring of a Virgin's womb!
Veiled in flesh the Godhead see,
Hail the incarnate Deity!
Pleased as Man with men to dwell,
Jesus, our Immanuel.

3 Hail, the heavenly Prince of Peace!
Hail, the Sun of Righteousness!
Light and life to all He brings,
Risen with healing in His wings.
Mild He lays His glory by,
Born that man no more may die,
Born to raise the sons of earth,
Born to give them second birth.

WM. AUSTIN.   A. S. SULLIVAN.

mf Moderato.

1. All this night bright angels sing, Never was such caroling, Hark! a voice which loudly cries,
2. Wake, O earth! wake every thing, Wake and hear the joy I bring; Wake and joy, for all this night,

Cres.   *f*   *p*   Cres.

"Mortals, mortals, wake and rise. Lo! to gladness Turns your sadness From the earth is
Heaven and every twinkling light, All amazing Still stand gazing, Angels, powers and

f   *p* 3d Verse.

ris'n a Sun, Shines all night, tho' day be done." Hail, O Sun! O blessed Light! Sent into this
all that be, Wake, and joy this Sun to see.

mf   Dim.   *pp*   Cres.

world by night; Let Thy rays and heav'nly pow'rs, Shine in these dark souls of ours. For most du-

f   *ff*   Rall.

ly, Thou art truly God and man, we do confess: Hail, O Sun of Righteousness!

CAROL.

1. Christ was born on Christmas day; Wreathe the holly, twine the bay;

CHRISTUS NATUS HO-DI-E; The Babe, the Son, the Ho-ly ONE of Ma-ry.

2 He is born to set us free,
He is born our Lord to be,
Ex Maria Virgine:
The God, the Lord, by all adored
    forever.

3 Let the bright red berries glow
Everywhere in goodly show,

Christus natus hodie:
The Babe, the Son, the Holy One of
    Mary.

4 Christian men, rejoice and sing,
'Tis the birthday of a King,
Ex Maria Virgine;
The God, the Lord, by all adored
    forever.

5. Night of sadness; morn of gladness, Ev-er-more: Ev-er, Ev-er:

Aft-er ma-ny troubles sore, Morn of gladness, evermore and ev-ermore.

6. Midnight scarcely passed and o-ver, Draw-ing to this ho-ly morn,

Ve - ry ear - ly, ve - ry ear - ly, Christ was born.

7. Sing out with bliss, His name is this: Em - man - u - el:

As was fore - told in days of old By Ga - bri - el.

ONCE IN ROYAL DAVID'S CITY.

C. F. ALEXANDER.　　　　　　　　　　　H. J. GAUNTLETT.

1. { Once in roy - al Da-vid's cit - y Stood a low - ly cat-tle shed, }
　{ Where a mother laid her Ba - by In a man - ger for His bed: }

Ma - ry was that mother mild, Je - sus Christ her lit-tle child. A-men.

He came down to earth from heaven,
　Who is God and Lord of all,
And His shelter was a stable,
　And His cradle in a stall;
　With the poor, and mean, and lowly,
　Lived on earth our Savior holy.

And our eyes at last shall see Him,
　Through His own redeeming love,
For that child so dear and gentle
　Is our Lord in heaven above;

And He leads His children on
　To the place where He is gone.

4 Not in that poor lowly stable,
　With the oxen standing by,
We shall see Him; but in heaven,
　Set at God's right hand on high;
　When like stars His children crowned,
　All in white shall wait around.
　　　　　　　　　　Amen.

E. W. KELLOGG. CAROL. J. H. HOPKINS, JR.

1. We three Kings of O - rient are, Bear-ing gifts we traverse a - far;

Field and fount-ain, Moor and mountain, Following yon - der Star.

CHORUS.

O Star of Wonder, Star of Night, Star with Roy-al Beauty bright,

Westward lead-ing, Still pro-ceed-ing, Guide us to Thy perfect light.

GASPARD.

2 Born a king on Bethlehem plain,
  Gold I bring to crown Him again;
    King forever,
    Ceasing never
  Over us all to reign.
  Chorus.—O Star, etc.

MELCHIOR.

3 Frankincense to offer have I,
  Incense owns a Deity nigh:
    Prayer and praising,
    All men raising,
  Worship Him, God on high.
  Chorus.—O Star, etc.

BALTHAZAR.

4 Myrrh is mine; its bitter perfume
  Breathes a life of gathering gloom
    Sorrowing, sighing,
    Bleeding, dying,
  Sealed in the stone-cold tomb
  Chorus.—O Star, etc.

5 Glorious now behold Him arise,
  King, and God, and Sacrifice;
    Heaven sings
    Hallelujah,
  Hallelujah, the earth replies.
  Chorus.—O Star, etc.

J. ELLERTON. ARTHUR SULLIVAN.

1. "Welcome, hap-py morning!" age to age shall say; Hell to-day is
2. Months in due suc-ces-sion, days of lengthening light, Hours and passing

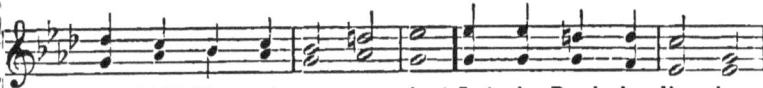

vanquish'd; Heaven is won to - day! Lo! the Dead is liv - ing,
mo-ments praise Thee in their flight; Brightness of the morn-ing,

God for e - vermore! Him their true Cre - a - tor, all His works a -
sky and fields and sea, Van-quish-er of darkness, bring their praise to

dore! "Welcome, happy morning!" age to age shall say. A - men.
Thee! "Welcome, happy morning!" age to age shall say.

3 Maker and Redeemer, Life and Health of all,
Thou from Heaven beholding human nature's fall,
Of the Father's Godhead true and only Son,
Manhood to deliver, Manhood didst put on:
Hell to-day is vanquished; Heaven is won to-day!

4 Thou, of Life the Author, death didst undergo,
Tread the path of darkness, saving strength to show;
Come then, True and Faithful, now fulfill Thy word;
'T is Thine own Third Morning! Rise, O buried Lord!
"Welcome, happy morning!" age to age shall say.

J. M. NEALE, tr.

ARTHUR SULLIVAN.

1. Come, ye faith-ful, raise the strain Of tri-umph-ant glad-ness;

God hath brought His Is-ra-el In-to joy from sad-ness:

Loosed from Pharaoh's bit-ter yoke, Ja-cob's sons and daugh-ters;

Led them with unmoistened foot Thro' the Red Sea wa-ters. A-men.

2 'Tis the Spring of souls to-day;
  Christ hath burst His prison;
And from three days' sleep in death
  As a sun hath risen:
All the winter of our sins,
  Long and dark, is flying
From His Light, to Whom we give
  Laud and praise undying.

3 Now the Queen of Seasons, bright
  With the day of splendor,
With the royal Feast of feasts,
  Comes its joy to render;

Comes to glad Jerusalem,
  Who with true affection,
Welcomes in unwearied strains
  Jesus' Resurrection.

4 Alleluia now we cry
  To our King Immortal,
Who triumphant burst the bars
  Of the tomb's dark portal;
Alleluia, with the Son
  God the Father praising;
Alleluia yet again
  To the Spirit raising. Amen.

E. H. SEARS.   CHRISTMAS CAROL.   J.

1. It came up - on the midnight clear, That glorious song of old,

From an-gels bend-ing near the earth, To touch their harps of gold;

"Peace on the earth, good will to men, From heav'n's all-gracious King."

The world in sol-emn still-ness lay, To hear the an - gels sing.

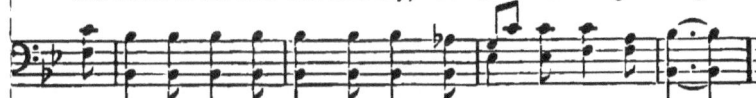

Still through the cloven skies they come,
With peaceful wings unfurled;
nd still their heavenly music floats
O'er all the weary world:
bove its sad and lowly plains
They bend on hovering wing,
nd ever o'er its Babel sounds
The blessed angels sing.

But with the woes of sin and strife
The world has suffered long;
eneath the angel-strain have rolled
Two thousand years of wrong;
nd man, at war with man, hears not
The love song which they bring;
h, hush the noise, ye men of strife,
And hear the angels sing.

4 And ye, beneath life's crushing load,
Whose forms are bending low,
Who toil along the climbing way,
With painful steps and slow,—
Look now; for glad and golden hours
Come swiftly on the wing:
Oh, rest beside the weary road,
And hear the angels sing.

5 For lo, the days are hastening on
By prophet bards foretold,
When with the ever-circling years
Comes round the age of gold;
When Peace shall over all the earth
Its ancient splendors fling,
And the whole world give back the song
Which now the angels sing.

I LOVE THE HOLY ANGELS.

STAINER.

1. I love the Ho - ly An - gels, So beau - ti - ful and bright;
2. 'Tis God, our Heavenly Fa - ther, Who doth the an - gels send,

And though I can not see them, They're with me day and night;
To guard His lit - tle chil-dren Un - til their life shall end.

They watch a-round my bed - side, They see me at my play;
When we are cross and naugh-ty, The Ho - ly An - gels grieve,

They know my ev - 'ry ac - tion, They hear the words I say.
For they are sad when children The way of goodness leave. A-men.

3 And when I die, the angels
    Will bear my soul away,
While here my body resteth
    Until the judgment day.
They'll bear me gently, softly,
    With loving care most sweet,
And lay me down in safety
    At my Redeemer's feet.

4 There with the Holy Angels,
    And holy men of old,
And all good friends who loved me,
    Too many to be told,
Shall I be with the angels,
    And all that people bright,
Forever and forever,
    In God's most glorious light.

MISS HANKEY. WM. G. FISCHER.

1. I love to tell the sto - ry Of un - seen things a - bove, Of
2. I love to tell the sto - ry, More won-der - ful it seems Than

Je - sus and His glo - ry, Of Je - sus and His love. I love to tell the
all the gold-en fan-cies Of all our golden dreams. I love to tell the

sto - ry, Because I know it's true; It sat - is-fies my longings, As
sto - ry, It did so much for me! And that is just the rea-son I

CHORUS.

nothing else can do. I love to tell the sto - ry, 'Twill be my theme in
tell it now to thee.

glo - ry, To tell the old, old sto - ry, Of Je - sus and His love.

3 I love to tell the story,
'Tis pleasant to repeat
What seems, each time I tell it,
More wonderfully sweet.
I love to tell the story,
For some have never heard
The message of salvation
From God's own holy word.

4 I love to tell the story,
For those who know it best
Seem hungering and thirsting
To hear it like the rest.
And when, in scenes of glory,
I sing the New, New Song,
'Twill be the Old, Old Story
That I have loved so long.

WM. WHITING.

1. Je - sus Christ, our Sav-ior, Once for us a child, In Thy whole be-

av - ior, Meek, o - be - dient, mild; In Thy foot-steps tread - ing,

We Thy lambs will be, Foe nor danger dreading, While we follow Thee.

2 For all Thou bestowest,
　All Thou dost withhold
Whatsoe'er Thou knowest
　Best for us, Thy fold.
For all gifts and graces
　While we live below,
Till in heavenly places
　We Thy face shall know.

3 We, Thy children, raising
　Unto Thee our hearts,
In Thy constant praising
　Bear our duteous parts,

As Thy love hath won us
　From the world away,
Still Thy hands put on us;
　Bless us day by day.

Let Thine angels guide us;
　Let Thine arms enfold;
In Thy bosom hide us,
　Sheltered from the cold;
To Thyself us gather,
　'Mid the ransomed host,
Praising Thee, the Father,
　And the Holy Ghost.

HARK, HARK, MY SOUL.

F. W. FABER.

H. SMART.

1. Hark! hark, my soul; Angelic songs are swelling O'er earth's green fields and
2. Onward we go, for still we hear them singing, "Come, weary souls, for
3. Far, far a - way, like bells at evening peal - ing, The voice of Je - sus
4. Rest comes at length, tho' life be long and dreary, The day must dawn, and
5. Angels, sing on! your faithful watches keeping; Sing us sweet fragments

ocean's wave-beat shore, How sweet the truth those blessed strains are telling
Jesus bids you come;" And, through the dark its echoes sweetly ring - ing,
sounds o'er land and sea, And laden souls by thousands meekly steal - ing,
darksome night be past; Faith's journey ends in welcome to the wea - ry,
of the songs above; Till morning's joy shall end the night of weep-ing,

CHORUS.

Of that new life when sin shall be no more.
The mu-sic of the Gospel leads us home. Angels of Je-sus, an - gels of
Kind Shepherd, turn their weary steps to Thee.
And heaven, the heart's true home, will come at last.
And life's long shadows break in cloudless love.

light, Sing-ing to wel - come the pilgrims of the night, Sing-ing to

wel - come the pilgrims, the pilgrims of the night. A - men, A - men.

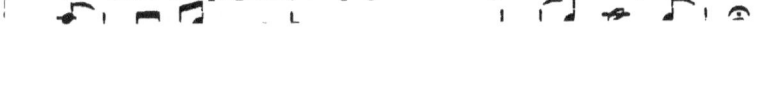

H. F. LYTE.   J. P. HOLBROOK, by per.

1. Praise, my soul, the King of heaven, To His feet thy tribute bring; Ransom'd,

healed, re-stored, for-giv-en, Ev-er-more His prais-es sing; Al - le -

lu - ia!   Al - le - lu - ia! Praise the ev - er - last-ing King.

2 Praise Him for His grace and favor
   To our fathers in distress;
Praise Him still the same as ever,
   Slow to chide and swift to bless;
      Alleluia! Alleluia!
Glorious in His faithfulness.

3 Father-like, He tends and spares us,
   Well our feeble frame He knows;
In His hands He gently bears us,
   Rescues us from all our foes;
      Alleluia! Alleluia!
Widely yet His mercy flows.

4 Angels in the height, adore Him;
   Ye behold Him face to face;
Saints, triumphant bow before Him,
   Gathered in from every race;
      Alleluia! Alleluia!
Praise with us the God of grace.

DOXOLOGY.

1 Praise and honor to the Father,
   Praise and honor to the Son,
Praise and honor to the Spirit,
   Ever Three and ever One:
One in might, and one in glory,
   While eternal ages run.

T. R. TAYLOR.   SULLIVAN.

1. We are but strangers here, Heaven is our Home; Earth is a desert drear, Heaven is our Home.

Danger and sorrow stand, Round us on every hand, Heaven is our Fa-ther-land, Heaven is our Home. A-men.

2 What though the tempests rage?
  Heaven is our Home;
Short is our pilgrimage,
  Heaven is our Home.
And Time's wild wintry blast
Soon shall be overpast,
We shall reach Home at last;
  Heaven is our Home.

3 There at our Savior's side,
  Heaven is our Home;
May we be glorified;
  Heaven is our Home.
There are the good and blest,
Those we love most and best,
Grant us with them to rest:
  Heaven is our Home. Amen.

JESUS STILL LEAD ON.

NICOLAUS LUDWIG ZINZENDORF   DRESE.

1. Jesus, still lead on, Till our rest be won; And altho' the way be cheerless,

We will follow, calm and fearless: Guide us by Thy Hand To our Fatherland.

"Jesu, geh voran."

2   If the way be drear,
    If the foe be near,
Let not faithless fears o'ertake us,
Let not faith and hope forsake us;
    For, through many a foe,
    To our home we go.

3   When we seek relief
    From a long-felt grief,
When temptations come alluring,

  Make us patient and enduring;
    Show us that bright shore
    Where we weep no more.

4   Jesus, still lead on,
    Till our rest be won;
Heavenly Leader, still direct us,
Still support, console, protect us,
    Till we safely stand
    In our Fatherland.

I LOVE TO THINK OF HEAVEN.

WM. PEARCE.   BEETHOVEN.

(Amen.)

1 I love to think of heaven, it seems not | far a- | way,
Its crystal streams refresh me as I | near the | closing | day;
Its balmy winds are wafted from the heavenly | hill a- | bove,
And they fold me in an atmosphere of | puri- | ty and | love.

2 I love to think of heaven, I long to | join the | choir,
To sing the song of Jesus my | soul would | never | tire;
The loved ones gone before me are joining | in the | song,
They cast their crowns before the Lamb who | sits up- | on the | throne.

3 I love to think of heaven, where the weary | are at | rest;
No sorrow there can enter to the | mansions | of the | blest;
All tears are wiped away by the Savior's | loving | hand,
And sin and death are banished from that | glorious | happy | land.

4 I love to think of heaven, and the greetings | I shall | meet
From the loving band of loved ones, who | walk the | golden | street;
And the patriarchs and prophets, I shall know them | every | one;
It is written in the Word, "we shall | know as | we are | known."

5 But oh, the rapturous vision when our eyes be- | hold the | King,
And hear the thrilling welcome, "Ye | blessed, | enter | in!"
Ten thousand suns encircle Him, ten thousand | crowns a- | dorn
The sacred head that bowed in death--the | head once | crowned with | thorns.

6 Assemble, all ye hosts, ye thrones, do- | minions, | powers!
There is no King like Jesus! there | is no | heaven like | ours!
All glory, hallelujah! let heaven and | earth u- | nite
To celebrate His praises with | infin- | ite de- | light. Amen.

THE GOLDEN LADDER.

1 I am climbing | up the | ladder
That | leads | to | Thee;
Oh, lend Thy | helping | hand
To | stead- | y | me.

2 I am weak and | can not | walk
Un- | aided | and a- | lone,
But Thy great | mercy | hast
Through | a- | ges | shone;

3 And I know that | with Thy | help
That | I | can | come,
Tho' the road be | dark and | thorny,
Up | to | my | home.

4 Do not let me | fall, O | Lord!
Keep | Thou | near | me;
So when cold | death doth | come,
I'll | keep | near | Thee.

F. W. FABER.   J. BARNBY.

1. O Par - a - dise! O Par - a - dise! Who doth not crave for rest?
2. O Par - a - dise! O Par - a - dise! The world is growing old;
3. O Par - a - dise! O Par - a - dise! Wherefore doth death delay?
4. O Par - a - dise! O Par - a - dise! 'Tis wea-ry wait-ing here;

Who would not seek the hap - py land Where they that loved, are blest?
Who would not be at rest and free Where love is nev - er cold?
Bright death that is the welcome dawn Of our e - ter - nal day;
I long to be where Je - sus is, To feel, to see Him near:

Where loyal hearts and true,

Where loy - al hearts and true, Stand ev - er in the light,

All rapture thro' and thro'. In God's most ho - ly sight. A - men.

JERUSALEM, THE GOLDEN.

J. M. NEALE.

EWING.

1. Je - ru - sa - lem, the gol - den! With milk and hon - ey blest;

Be - neath Thy con - tem - pla - tion Sink heart and voice op - prest;

I know not, oh! I know not What joys a - wait us there;

What ra - di - ancy of glo - ry, What bliss beyond compare. A - men.

2 They stand, those halls of Zion,
   All jubilant with song,
And bright with many an angel,
   And all the martyr throng;
The Prince is ever in them,
   The daylight is serene;
The pastures of the blessed
   Are decked in glorious sheen.

3 There is the throne of David,
   And there, from care released,
The shout of them that triumph,
   The song of them that feast.
And they, who, with their Leader,
   Have conquered in the fight,
Forever and forever
   Are clad in robes of white.

J. M. NEALE, tr.

J. P. HOLBROOK, by per.

1. For thee, O dear, dear coun-try, Mine eyes their vig-ils keep;

For ver-y love be-hold-ing Thy hap-py name, they weep.

The men-tion of Thy glo-ry Is unc-tion to the breast,

And med-i-cine in sick-ness, And love, and life, and rest.

2 O one, O only mansion!
  O Paradise of joy!
Where tears are ever banished,
  And smiles have no alloy;
The Lamb is all Thy splendor,
  The Crucified Thy praise:
His laud and benediction
  Thy ransomed people raise.

3 O sweet and blessed country,
  The home of God's elect!
O sweet and blessed country,
  That eager hearts expect!
Jesus, in mercy bring us
  To that dear land of rest:
Who art, with God the Father,
  And Spirit ever blest. Amen.

HOSANNA WE SING.

English.

1. Ho - san - na we sing, like the chil - dren dear, In the
2. Ho - san - na we sing, for He bends His ear, And re-

old - en days when the Lord lived here; He bless'd lit-tle children, and
joices the hymns of His own to hear; We know that His heart will

smiled on them, While they chanted His praise in Je - ru - sa - lem.
nev-er wax cold To the lambs that He feeds in His earth - ly fold.

Al - le - lu - ia we sing, like the chil -dren bright, With their
Al - le - lu - ia we sing in the church we love, Al - le-

harps of gold, and their raiment white, As they follow their Shepherd with
lu-ia resounds in the church a - bove; To Thy little ones, Lord, may such

lov-ing eyes, Thro' the beautiful valleys of Par - a - dise.
grace be giv'n,That we lose not our part in the song of heav'n. A-men.

WE ARE LITTLE PILGRIMS.

HULLAH.

In Unison.

1. We are lit - tle pil - grims, We are stran-gers here;
2. Oft-times we are wea - ry, Oft - en - times in pain;

We are hast'ning on - ward To our home most dear.
But the hope of heav - en Cheers our souls a - gain.

Harmony. **Rall.**

All that stays our pro - gress We will cast a - side,
Grief will there be rapt - ure, Toil will there be rest;

A tempo. **Rall.**

Sin - ful lusts and pas-sions, E - vil thoughts and pride.
Each day brings us near - er To our home most blest. A - men.

CESAR MALAN.

1. Heavenly Fa - ther, hear our prayer, Offered through Thy Ho - ly Son;

Evening shadows fill the air; Day, with all its cares, is done.

Soon shall sleep our eye - lids close, Let our souls on Thee re - pose;

Rit.

Soon shall sleep our eye - lids close, Let our souls on Thee re - pose.

2 Lord, Thou knowest all our ways—
  All our life is in Thy hand;
Few and evil are our days,
  Soon cut off at Thy command—
Like a flower, at morning bright,
Broken, withered, ere the night;
Like a flower, at morning bright,
Broken, withered, ere the night.

3 Keep us, Lord, while here we stay,
  Safe beneath Thy sheltering wing;
Let our nightly rest, we pray,
  Strength for daily labor bring.
Ever guide us, till at last
Earthly nights and days are past;
Ever guide us, till at last
Earthly nights and days are past.

TRANQUIL AND PEACEFUL.

FLEMMING.

1. Tranquil and peaceful is the path to heaven, Where now so many fresh from earth's ripe
2. There life is blissful! shall the spirit tremble? Bright heavenly angels wait to lead us
3. There our lost rosebuds in our hands shall open; Love, pure and holy, in our bosoms

vintage; So many happy, high and blessed spirits Wait to receive us.
yonder, There dwell the spirits purified by suffering, Blessing and blessed.
glowing, Flows from the Father, source of every blessing, Living and loving.

COME, OH, COME TO JESUS.

H. C. CAMP. By per.

1. Sinner, come! 'Mid thy gloom, All thy guilt confessing; Trembling now, Contrite bow,

CHORUS.

Take the of-fered blessing. Come to Je - sus now! Come to Je - sus

now! Come to Je - sus, He will save you; Come, oh, come to Je - sus.

2 Sinner, come!
While there's room,
While the feast is waiting;
While the Lord,
By His word,
Kindly is inviting.

3 Sinner, come,
Ere thy doom
Shall be sealed forever;
Now return,
Grieve and mourn,
Flee to Christ, the Savior.

4 Come, believe,
Oh, receive
Peace that like a river
Flows for thee
Pure and free;
Drink and live forever.

"HE KNOWETH THE WAY THAT I TAKE."

J. P. Holbrook.

1. I know not—the way is so mist - y— The joys or the
2. I stand where the cross-roads are meet-ing, And know not the
3. And I know that the way leadeth home-ward To the land of the

griefs it may bring, What clouds are o'erhang-ing the fut - ure, What
right from the wrong; No beck - on - ing fin-gers di - rect me, No
pure and the blest, To the coun-try of ev - er - fair sum-mer, To the

flow'rs by the road-side shall spring; But there's One who will journey be-
wel - come floats to me in song; But my guide will soon give me a
cit - y of peace and of rest; And there shall be heal-ing for

side me, Nor in weal nor in woe will for - sake; And this is my
tok - en By wil - der-ness, mountain, or lake— What-ev - er the
sick -ness, And fountains, life's fe - ver to slake. What matters be-

sol - ace and com - fort— "He knoweth the way that I take."
dark - ness a - bout me, "He knoweth the way that I take."
side? I go heav'n-ward— "He knoweth the way that I take."

DAILY WORK.

S. S. Hymnal, by per. Rev. E. P. Parker.

1. In the vine-yard of our Fa-ther, Dai-ly work we find to do;
2. Toiling ear - ly in the morn-ing; Catching moments thro' the day;

Scat-tered gleanings we may gath-er, Tho' we are but young and few.
Noth-ing small or low-ly scorn-ing While we work, and watch, and pray.

Lit - tle clus-ters, Lit - tle clus-ters, Help to fill the gar-ners too.
Gath'ring glad-ly, Gath'ring glad-ly, Free-will off'rings by the way.

t for selfish praise or glory;
Not for objects nothing worth;
t to send the blessed story
Of the Gospel o'er the earth,
ling mortals, Telling mortals
Of our Lord and Savior's birth.

4 Steadfast, then, in our endeavor,
   Heavenly Father, may we be;
And forever and forever
   We will give the praise to Thee.
Hallelujah, Hallelujah,
   Singing, all eternity.

SONG OF THE LITTLE WORKERS.

JESSE CLEMENT.   JAMES MCGRANAHAN.

1. A band of hum-ble workers In the vineyard of the Lord, We,
2. Since Christ, the good examplar, Did i - dle-ness up-braid, The

like the blessed Savior, Will strive in sweet accord, To do the Master's
hands that covet la-bor Shall have our cheerful aid; The homeless and for-

bid-ding, Whate'er the task assigned, Our rallying song and watchword, "The
sak - en, We'll help to safe retreats, Where skies are never frowning, And

good of human kind." The good of human kind, The good of hu-man
tempests nev-er beat. And tempests nev-er beat, And tempests nev - er

kind. Our rallying song and watchword, "The good of human kind."
beat. Where skies are nev - er frown-ing, And tempests nev - er beat.

SUPPLICATION.

From 8. 8. Hymnal, by per.

1. Heavenly Fa-ther, from Thy throne, Look in love and pit - y down;
2. By the great and ten-der love Thou didst once for sin - ners prove,

Thou canst save, and Thou a - lone; Lord, in mer - cy hear us.
Love that brought Thee from a-bove; Je - sus, Sav - ior, hear us.

Blessed Spirit, gentle Dove,
From Thy home in heaven above,
Come, and fill our hearts with love,
Holy Spirit, hear us.

4 When our feet are led to stray
From Thy pure and perfect way,
Then, withhold us, Lord, we pray;
Jesus, Savior, hear us.

MORE LOVE TO THEE, O CHRIST.

E. P. PRENTISS.　　　　　　J. P. HOLBROOK. By per.

1. More love to Thee, O Christ! More love to Thee! Hear Thou the pray'r I make, On bended

Rit.

knee; This is my earnest plea—More love, O Christ, to Thee, More love to Thee.

2 Once earthly joy I craved,
　Sought peace and rest;
Now Thee alone I seek,
　Give what is best:
This all my prayer shall be—
More love, O Christ, to Thee,
　More love to Thee.

3 Let sorrow do its work,
　Send grief and pain;
Sweet are Thy messengers,
　Sweet their refrain,

When they can sing with me—
More love, O Christ, to Thee,
　More love to Thee.

4 Then shall my latest breath
　Whisper Thy praise;
This be the parting cry
　My heart shall raise,—
This still its prayer shall be—
More love, O Christ, to Thee,
　More love to Thee.

LITTLE CHILDREN, COME TO JESUS.

1. Little children, come to Jesus; Hear Him saying, come to me:
Blessed Jesus, Who to save us, Shed His blood on Calvary. } Little souls were made to

serve Him; All His holy law fulfill: Little hearts were made to love Him; Little hands to do His will. Amen

2 Little eyes to read the Bible,
  Given from the heavens above;
Little ears to hear the story
  Of the Savior's wondrous love;

Little tongues to sing His praises;
  Little feet to walk His ways;
Little bodies to be temples
  Where the Holy Spirit stays. Amen

THE LOVING LITTLE ONES.

REV. E. UNANGST.   J. H. KURZENKNABE.

1. 'T is Jesus loves the little ones, and calls them as His own, He's always with the
2. Let little ones sing Jesus' name, He loves to hear them sing, And fill His courts with

The lov - ing   little ones, The
CHORUS.

little ones, They're never left alone. The loving, loving little ones, The
joyful sound, And make His praises ring.

love - ly   little ones, The bless-ed   little ones, The happy little ones.

lovely, lovely little ones, The blessed, blessed little ones, The happy little ones.

3 He loves to be with little ones,
  And hear their childlike prayer,
And tenderly He takes them up,
  Into His loving care.

4 'T is Jesus whom the little ones
  May call their loving king;
'T is He that makes them angels, too,
  His name for aye to sing.

help you Some oth-er to win; Fight man-ful - ly on - ward,
rev-'rence, Nor take it in vain; Be thoughtful and car - nest,
con - quer, Though often cast down; He who is our Sav - ior,

Dark passions subdue, Look ev-er to Je - sus, He'll carry you through.
Kind-hearted and true, Look ev-er to Je - sus, He'll carry you through.
Our strength will renew, Look ev-er to Je - sus, He'll carry you through.

CHORUS.

Ask the Sav - ior to help you, Com - fort, strengthen and keep you;

WORK.

Mrs. BELLE TOWNE.　　　　　　　　　　　　　　　　　T. MARTIN TOWNE.

1. Work, work! *where* shall we work, Where is the field we may share?
2. Work, work! *how* shall we work, How shall we la-bor a - right?
3. Work, work! *when* shall we work, When shall the sickle go in?
4. Work, work! ev - er we'll work, Working with hearts full of love;

Ev - er in sight is the harvest white, Work can be found any where.
Working in love like the angels a - bove, Working with God in our might.
Working *to - day* is the on - ly way, If a full harvest we'd win.
Working in might with the morning light, Working for Jesus a - bove.

CHORUS.

Work! work, work! Ev - er we'll work, work for the Lord;

Haste, haste, haste! Lin - ger not, time wait-eth for none.

. By permission of STILLMAN & TOWNE.

National Hymn of Holland.

From S. S. Hymnal, by per.

1. All glo-ry in the high - est Be giv - en, Lord, to Thee;

On earth, with men of good - will, Let peace for - ev - er be.

We praise Thee, we a - dore Thee, We bless and mag - ni - fy;

And for Thine own great glo - ry, We thank Thee, Lord, most

high, We thank Thee, Lord, most high.

2 And Thou, O Christ, our Savior,
    God's well-beloved Son;
  O Jesus, our anointed,
    Who hast redemption won;
  Thou for the world's transgressions
    Dost evermore atone;
  O Lamb, who guilt absolvest,
    To us be mercy shown.

WE PLOW THE FIELDS AND SCATTER.

SCHULTZ.

1. We plow the fields and scat-ter The good seed on the land, But
2. He on - ly is the Mak - er Of all things near and far; He
3. We thank Thee, then, O Fa - ther, For all things bright and good, The

it is fed and watered By God's al-might-y hand. He sends the snow in
paints the wayside flow-er, He lights the evening star. The winds and waves o-
seed-time and the harvest, Our life, our health, our food. Accept the gifts we

winter, The warmth to swell the grain, The breezes and the sunshine, And
bey Him, By Him the birds are fed; Much more to us, His children, He
of - fer, For all Thy love im-parts, And, what Thou most desirest, Our

CHORUS.

soft, re-freshing rain.
gives our dai-ly bread. All good gifts around us, Are sent from heav'n above,
humble, thankful hearts.

HENRY ALFORD.   G. J. ELVEY.

1. Come, ye thank-ful peo - ple, come, Raise the song of Harvest-home;
2. All the world is God's own field, Fruit un - to His praise to yield;

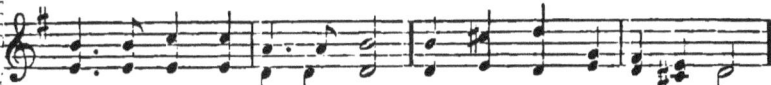

All is safe - ly gath-ered in, Ere the win - ter storms be-gin;
Wheat and tares to-geth - er sown, Un - to joy or sor - row grown;

God, our Mak - er, doth pro - vide For our wants to be sup-plied;
First the blade, and then the ear, Then the full corn shall ap - pear;

Come to God's own tem - ple, come, Raise the song of Harvest - home.
Lord of Har-vest, grant that we Wholesome grain and pure may be.

3 For the Lord our God shall come,
And shall take His harvest home;
From His field shall in that day
All offences purge away;
Give His angels charge at last
In the fire the tares to cast;
But the fruitful ears to store
In His garner evermore.

4 Even so, Lord, quickly come
To Thy final Harvest-home;
Gather Thou Thy people in,
Free from sorrow, free from sin;
There, forever purified,
In Thy presence to abide;
Come, with all Thine angels, come,
Raise the glorious Harvest-home.

WORDS ARE THINGS OF LITTLE COST.

1. Words are things of lit - tle cost, Quick-ly spok - en, quickly lost;

We for - get them, but they stand Wit - ness - es at God's right hand,

And their tes - ti - mo - ny bear For us, or a-gainst us there. A-men.

2 Oh, how often ours have been
Idle words and words of sin!
Words of anger, scorn, or pride,
Or deceit, our faults to hide,
Envious tales, or strife unkind,
Leaving bitter thoughts behind.

3 Grant us, Lord, from day to day,
Strength to watch, and grace to pray,
May our lips from sin kept free,
Love to speak and sing of Thee;
Till in heaven we learn to raise
Hymns of everlasting praise. Amen.

BE NEAR US.

Rev. E. P. Parker.
From S. S. Hymnal, by per.

1. When the world is bright-est, When our hearts are light - est,
2. When life's scene is shad - ed, All its bright hopes fad - ed,

Bless - ed Je - sus, hear: Let Thy help be near.
Bless - ed Je - sus, hear: Light of heaven, be near.

3 When our foes surround us,
When our sins have bound us,
Blessed Jesus, hear,
Let Thy help be near.

4 When life, slowly waning,
Shows but heaven remaining,
Blessed Jesus, hear:
Light of heaven, be near.

Mrs. M. J. BITTLE.

J. H. FILLMORE. By per.

1. Long a - go, in old Ju - de - a, By the shores of Gal - i - lee,

Je - sus spake un - to the fish-ers: "Leave your nets and follow me."

Lit - tle chil - dren, hear the sto-ry, Peal-ing thro' the ag - es dim;

Who of you will leave your pleasures, Take your cross and follow Him?

2 Now no more in old Judea,
  Jesus walketh by the sea;
But He calleth, ever calleth,
  Who will come and follow me?
Come to Jesus—time may tarnish
  Many a dream of beauty fair;
What He offers, fadeth never
  Life eternal over there.

3 Over there, beyond death's billows,
  Eyes of faith can plainly see
The bright mansions where He promised
  All His followers should be.
Children, listen to the story,
  Pealing thro' the ages dim;
Jesus loves you! died to save you!
  Give up all, and follow Him.

JESUS, I LIVE TO THEE.

H. HARBAUGH.   J. P. HOLBROOK, by per.

1. Je - sus, I live to Thee, The love - li - est and best;

My life in Thee, Thy life in me, In Thy blest love I rest.

Copyright, 1881, by J. P. HOLBROOK.

1 Jesus, I live to Thee,
  The loveliest and best,
  My life in Thee, Thy life in me,
  In Thy blest love I rest.

2 Jesus, I die to Thee,
  Whenever death shall come;
  To die in Thee is life to me,
  In my eternal home.

3 Whether to live or die,
  I know not which is best;
  To live in Thee is bliss to me,
  To die is endless rest.

4 Living or dying, Lord,
  I ask but to be thine;
  My life in Thee, Thy life in me,
  Makes heaven forever mine.

1 Blest be Thy love, dear Lord,
  That taught us this sweet way,
  Only to love Thee for Thyself
  And for that love obey.

2 O Thou, our souls' chief hope,
  We to Thy mercy fly;
  Where'er we are, Thou canst protect,
  Whate'er we need, supply.

3 Whether we sleep or wake,
  To Thee we both resign;
  By night we see, as well as day,
  If Thy light on us shine.

4 Whether we live or die,
  Both we submit to Thee;
  In death we live, as well as life,
  If Thine in death we be.

                                    J. AUSTIN.

TOPLADY.

DR. T. HASTINGS.

Fine.

1. Rock of A - ges, cleft for me, Let me hide my - self in thee!
D. C. Be of sin the double cure; Cleanse me from its guilt and power.

D. C.

Let the wa - ter and the blood, From His riv - en side that flow'd,

A. M. TOPLADY. J. P. HOLBROOK, by per.

1. Rock of A - ges, cleft for me, Let me hide my - self in thee!
2. Not the la - bor of my hands Can ful - fill the law's demands;

Let the wa - ter and the blood, From Thy wound-ed side that flowed,
Could my zeal no res - pite know, Could my tears for - ev - er flow,

Be of sin the doub-le cure; Cleanse me from its guilt and power.
All for sin could not a - tone, Thou must save, and Thou a - lone.

Rock of A - ges, cleft for me, Let me hide my - self in thee.
Rock of A - ges, cleft for me, Let me hide my - self in thee.

3 Nothing in my hand I bring,
Simply to Thy cross I cling;
Naked, come to Thee for dress;
Helpless, look to Thee for grace;
Vile, I to the fountain fly,
Wash me, Savior, or I die!
Rock of Ages, cleft for me,
Let me hide myself in thee.

4 While I draw this fleeting breath,
When my eyelids close in death,
When I soar to worlds unknown,
See Thee on Thy judgment-throne,
Rock of Ages, cleft for me!
Let me hide myself in thee.
Rock of Ages, cleft for me,
Let me hide myself in thee.

STAND UP, STAND UP FOR JESUS.

Rev. Geo. Duffield.   G. J. Webb.

1. Stand up, stand up for Je - sus, Ye sol - diers of the cross;

Lift high His roy - al ban - ner, It must not suf - fer loss;
D.S. Till ev - 'ry foe is vanquished, And Christ is Lord in - deed.

From victory un - to vic - tory His ar - my He shall lead,

2 Stand up, stand up for Jesus,
    The trumpet call obey;
Forth to the mighty conflict,
    In this His glorious day:
"Ye that are men, now serve Him
    Against unnumbered foes;
Your courage rise with danger,
    And strength to strength oppose.

3 Stand up, stand up for Jesus,
    Stand in His strength alone;
The arm of flesh will fail you·
    Ye dare not trust your own:
Put on the gospel armor,
    And watching unto prayer,
Where duty calls, or danger,
    Be never wanting there.

4 Stand up, stand up for Jesus,
    The strife will not be long;
This day the noise of battle,
    The next the victor's song:
To him that overcometh
    A crown of life shall be;
He with the King of glory
    Shall reign eternally.

1 The morning light is breaking;
    The darkness disappears;
The sons of earth are waking
    To penitential tears;
Each breeze that sweeps the ocean
    Brings tidings from afar
Of nations in commotion,
    Prepared for Zion's war.

2 See heathen nations bending
    Before the God we love,
And thousand hearts ascending,
    In gratitude above;
While sinners, now confessing,
    The gospel call obey,
And seek the Savior's blessing,
    A nation in a day.

3 Blest river of salvation,
    Pursue thine onward way;
Flow thou to every nation,
    Nor in thy riches stay:
Stay not, till all the lowly
    Triumphant reach their home;
Stay not, till all the holy
    Proclaim, "The Lord is come."

Rev. S. F. Smith.

G. KEITH.   READING.

1. How firm a foun-da-tion, ye saints of the Lord, Is laid for your

faith in His ex-cel-lent word! What more can He say than to

you He hath said,— To you who for ref-uge to Je-sus have

fled? To you who for ref-uge to Je-sus have fled?

2 "Fear not, I am with thee, oh, be not dismayed,
For I am thy God, I will still give thee aid;
I'll strengthen thee, help thee, and cause thee to stand,
Upheld by my righteous, omnipotent hand.

3 "When through the deep waters I call thee to go,
The rivers of sorrow shall not overflow;
For I will be with thee thy trials to bless,
And sanctify to thee thy deepest distress.

4 "The soul that on Jesus hath leaned for repose,
I will not—I will not desert to his foes;
That soul—though all hell should endeavor to shake,—
I'll never—no, never—no, never forsake!"

I WAS A WANDERING SHEEP.

BONAR.   ZUNDEL.

1. I was a wand'ring sheep, I did not love the fold,
2. The Shepherd sought His sheep, The Fa-ther sought His child;

I did not love my Shepherd's voice, I would not be con-trolled;
He fol-lowed me o'er vale and hill, O'er des-erts waste and wild;

I was a wayward child, I did not love my home,
He found me nigh to death, Famished, and faint, and lone;

I did not love my Father's voice, I loved a-far to roam.
He bound me with the bands of love, He saved the wand'ring one.

3 Jesus my Shepherd is;
   'Twas He that loved my soul,
'Twas He that washed me in His blood,
   'Twas He that made me whole;
'Twas He that sought the lost,
   That found the wandering sheep;
'Twas He that brought me to the fold,
   'Tis He that still doth keep.

4 No more a wandering sheep,
   I love to be controlled,
I love my tender Shepherd's voice,
   I love the peaceful fold.
No more a wayward child,
   I seek no more to roam;
I love my heavenly Father's voice,
   I love, I love His home!

C. GUONOD.

1. Who is this that comes from E - dom, All His
2. 'Tis the Sav - ior, now vic - to - rious, Travel-ing

rai - ment stained with blood, To the cap - tive speak - ing
on - ward in His might; 'Tis the Sav - ior, oh, how

free - dom, Bring - ing and be - stow - ing good? Glo - rious
glo - rious To His peo - ple is the sight! Sa - tan

is the garb He wears, Glo - rious is the spoil He bears.
con-quered and the grave; Je - sus now is strong to save.

3 This the Savior has effected
    By His mighty arm alone;
See the throne for Him erected;
    'Tis an everlasting throne.
'Tis the great reward He gains,
Glorious fruit of all His pains.

4 Mighty Victor! reign forever;
    Wear the crown so dearly won;
Never shall Thy people, never,
    Cease to sing what Thou hast done;
Thou hast fought Thy people's foes,
Thou hast healed Thy people's woes.

WHAT ARE THESE IN BRIGHT ARRAY.

JAMES MONTGOMERY.   E. IVES, JR.

1. What are these in bright ar-ray, This in-nu-mer-a-ble throng,

Round the al-tar night and day, Hymning one tri-umph-ant song:

D. S. Wisdom, rich-es, to ob-tain, New do-min-ion ev-'ry hour."

"Worthy is the Lamb, once slain, Blessing, hon-or, glo-ry, power,

2 These through fiery trials trod;
　These from great afflictions came;
Now, before the throne of God,
　Sealed with His Almighty Name;
Clad in raiment pure and white,
　Victor-palms in every hand,
Through their dear Redeemer's might,
　More than conquerors they stand.

3 Hunger, thirst, disease unknown,
　On immortal fruits they feed;
Them the Lamb amidst the throne,
　Shall to living fountains lead;
Joy and gladness banish sighs,
　Perfect love dispels all fear,
And forever from their eyes
　God shall wipe away the tear.

———

1 Palms of glory, raiment bright,
　Crowns that never fade away,
Gird and deck the saints in light,
　Priests, and kings, and conquerors they.

Yet the conquerors bring their palms
　To the Lamb amidst the throne,
And proclaim in joyful psalms,
　Victory through His cross alone.

2 Kings for harps their crowns resign,
　Crying, as they strike the chords,
"Take the kingdom, it is Thine,
　King of kings, and Lord of lords."
Round the altar, priests confess,
　If their robes are white as snow,
'T was the Savior's righteousness,
　And His blood, that made them so.

3 Who were these?—On earth they dwelt,
　Sinners once of Adam's race,
Guilt, and fear, and suffering felt,
　But were saved by sovereign grace.
They were mortal, too, like us:
　Ah, when we, like them, shall die,
May our souls, translated thus,
　Triumph, reign, and shine on high.

JAMES MONTGOMERY.

By per. of Rev. E. P. Parker.

1. There is a green hill far a-way, Without a cit-y wall,
2. We may not know, we can not tell What pain He had to bear;

Where the dear Lord was cru-ci-fied, And died to save us all.
But we be-lieve it was for us He hung and suffered there.

CHORUS.

Oh, dear-ly, dear-ly has He loved, And we must love Him too;

And trust in His re-deeming blood, And try His works to do.

3 He died that we might be forgiven,
    He died to make us good;
  That we might go at last to heaven,
    Saved by His precious blood.

4 There was no other good enough
    To pay the price of sin;
  He only could unlock the gate
    Of heaven, and let us in.

I WOULD LIVE LIKE JESUS.

Rev. E. P. Parker, by per.

1. I would live like Je - sus, Free from ev - 'ry sin;

May His Ho - ly Spir - it Make me pure with - in.

I would toil for Je - sus, Strengthened by His grace;

Till in end - less glo - ry I be - hold His face.

2 I would tell to Jesus
  Every grief and care,
He delights to answer
  Humble, fervent prayer.
Through the changeful future,
  Jesus, be my guide;
In Thy great compassion
  Keep me near Thy side.

3 I would trust in Jesus
  All my journey through;
He is ever faithful,
  He is ever true.
Savior, in my spirit
  Shed abroad Thy love;
When I die, receive me
  To Thy home above.

From Holbrook's Quartet and Chorus Choir, by per.

My spir - it longs for Thee, To dwell with-in my breast:

Al - though un - wor - thy I Of so di - vine a guest,

Of so di - vine a guest; Un - wor - thy though I be,

Yet hath my heart no rest Un - til it come to Thee.

BEAUTIFUL LAND OF REST.

From S. S. Hymnal, by per.

1. Je - ru - sa - lem, so bright and fair, Beau - ti - ful land of rest!
2. We long to see thy pearl - y gates, Beau - ti - ful land of rest!
3. Un - to the riv - er's banks we come, Beau - ti - ful land of rest!

No gloom-y night, nor sor-row there, Beau - ti - ful land of rest!
And for their open-ing still we wait, Beau - ti - ful land of rest!
Each moment brings us near-er home, Beau - ti - ful land of rest!

Je - sus, the Sun, for - ev - er reigns, O'er all those bright ce-les-tial plains,
And when our toils and cares are o'er, Then those who've crossed the stream before
There millions who've the vict'ry found, Have laid the cross and armor down,

And an - gels sing in joy - ful strains In the land of rest.
Will wel - come us to Canaan's shore, To the land of rest.
But we are striv-ing for the crown In the land of rest.

Miss Ellen H. Willis.   English.

1. I left it all with Je-sus, Long a-go; All my sins I brought Him,
2. I leave it all with Je-sus, For He knows How to steal the bit-ter

And my woe; When by faith I saw Him On the tree, Heard His small, still
From life's woes; How to gild the tear-drop With His smile, Make the desert

whis-per, 'Tis for thee; From my heart the bur-den Rolled a-way—
gar-den Bloom a-while; When my weakness lean-eth On His might,

Cres.   *Rit.*

Hap-py day! From my heart the burden Rolled a-way—Happy day!
All seems light. When my weakness leaneth On His might, All seems light.

3 I leave it all with Jesus
   Day by day;
Faith can firmly trust Him
   Come what may;
Hope has dropped her anchor,
   Found her rest,
In the calm, sure haven
   Of His breast;
‖: Love esteems it heaven
   To abide—At His side. :‖

4 Oh, leave it *all* with Jesus,
   Drooping soul!
Tell not *half* thy story,
   But the whole.
Worlds on worlds are hanging
   On His hand,
Life and death are waiting
   His command;
‖: Yet His tender bosom
   Makes *thee* room—Oh, come home. :‖

OH! THE JOY OF CALMLY RESTING.

J. W. S.

GREGOR SPECK.

Slow.

1. Oh! the joy of calm-ly rest - ing, On the Sav - ior's changeless

love: Oh! the sweetness thus of test-ing, Mer - cy flow - ing from a -

bove, When the heart from care is sink - ing, When the bo - som deep - ly

sighs; On His words of comfort thinking, Every load of trouble flies.

2 "Casting all thy care upon Him,"
  Is the Spirit's earnest call;
"On the Lord cast all thy burden,"
  Every weight of trial roll.
Though the path thy foot now presses,
  Straight across the desert lie,
Once that path was trod by Jesus,
  Every step of sorrow nigh.

3 Brief the period of thy sorrow,
  Strong His sympathy of love,
Endless is thy bright to-morrow,
  With Him in His courts above.
Nought thy soul from Him can sever
  Nought His love from thee can part
Thine His rest, His home forever,
  Thine His smile, His joy, His heart

Used by permission of O. Ditson & Co.

LUTHER JAMES.

T. MARTIN TOWNE, by per.

1. Look ye, broth - ers, time is roll-ing, Roll-ing rap - id - ly a - way;
2. Plant your stand-ard firm and fearless, On the cit - a - del of night;

Ves - per bells will soon be toll-ing, Tolling for the dy-ing day:
Hard may seem the task and cheerless, But the promis'd crown is bright:

Rouse thee, comrades, nerve for la - bor, In life's bat - tle, dare and do!
Poor yourself, you have for oth-ers Wealth, you may not, must not keep,

Bold - ly wield truth's gleaming saber, Vanquish wrong and right pursue.
Words of cheer for drooping brothers, Tears to shed with those who weep.

3 Smiles to cheer the lone one's labor,
Toiling o'er life's weary way;
Bread to share with poorer neighbors,
Hung'ring, starving, ev'ry day:
Go to hearts that pine and perish,
Wipe the flowing tears away;
Ev'ry smitten spirit nourish,
Drooping sadly by the way.

4 Carry gladness to the sighing,
Give your strength to bear the lame,
Whisper comfort to the dying,
Whisper softly Jesus' name:
Up some hill or down some valley,
Seek the lost to guide aright;
Hark! the bugle sounds the rally,
Gird you, comrades, for the fight.

JAMES PRICE.

1. We'll sing as we go through the val-ley be-low, And
2. We'll sing of the vic-to-ry Je-sus has won, We'll
3. We'll sing of the place He has gone to pre-pare, Up

while thro' the des-ert we roam; We'll sing in the midst of our
sing how He died on the tree; We'll sing of the glo-ri-ous
where the bright pearly gates stand, And all they that give themselves

tri-als and woe, Sweet songs of our beau-ti-ful home.
work He has done, Sal-va-tion for you and for me.
up to His care, Shall go to the beau-ti-ful land.

CHORUS.

Soon, soon, soon, Soon we shall reach the bright shore, And

join with the ransomed in glory a-bove, Then we shall sing ever-more.

UP YONDER.

MARGARETTE SNODGRASS.   T. MARTIN TOWNE. By per.

1. Tho' our pathway may be drear - y, Yon-der there is light;
2. Nev - er then de-spair or won - der; On - ly day by day,
3. One has trod the steps be - fore us, Marking all the way;

And a Hand when we are wea - ry, Reaching thro' the night.
As the darkness drifts a - sun - der, We shall find our way.
While His watchful care is o'er us, We need nev - er stray.

CHORUS.

There are worlds of light up yonder, There is al-ways light up yon-der,

In the darkest night; There are worlds of light, If we lift our eyes up yonder.

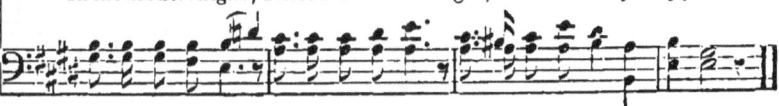

MIGHTY TO SAVE.

R. W. Todd,

Harry Sanders, by per.

1. Oh, who is this that com - eth From E - dom's crim-son plain,
2. Oh, why is thine ap - par - el With reek-ing gore all dyed,
3. O bleed - ing Lamb, my Sav - ior, How couldst Thou bear this shame?

With wounded side, with garments dyed? Oh, tell me now thy name.
Like them that tread the wine-press red? Oh, why this bloody tide?
"With mercy fraught, mine own arm brought Salva - tion in my name.

"I, that saw thy soul's dis - tress, A ran - som gave.
"I the wine-press trod a - lone, 'Neath dark'ning skies.
I the blood - y fight have won, Con-quered the grave.

I that speak in right-eous - ness, Might-y to save."
Of the peo - ple there was none Might-y to save."
Now the year of joy has come,—Might-y to save."

REFRAIN.

f Cres.

Might-y to save,.. Might-y to save,..
Might-y to save, Might-y to save,

ff

Might-y to save. Lord, I trust Thy wondrous love, Mighty to save.

CHRIST IN THE SHIP.

ALFORD.   REV. E. P. PARKER.

y bark is waft - ed   on the strand By breath di - vine;
e holds me when the   billows smite; I shall not fall;

id on the helm there rests a hand,   Oth - er than mine.
sharp, 'tis short; if   long, 'tis light; He tem - pers all.

ie who has known in storms to sail, I have on board;
fe to the land! safe to the land! The end is this;

. - bove the rag - ing of the gale, I hear my Lord.
.nd then with Him go hand in hand Far in - to bliss.

LITTLE BEAMS OF BRIGHTNESS.

Wm. Kibbey.

J. H. Fillmore. By per.

1. Lit - tle beams of bright-ness, Lit - tle gems of love,
2. And the lit - tle an - gels, Sing - ing as they roam,

Make the bliss - ful E - den Of the realms a - bove.
Make that land de - light - ful For a heaven-ly home.

3 So may little children,
As a little band,
Brighten every footstep
To the heavenly land.

4 Little prayers devoted,
Little songs of praise,
To our blessed Father
Brighten all our days.

5 Learning of the Savior,
Is the heavenly way,
Leading on to Glory,
And eternal day.

HEAR THE PENNIES DROPPING.

Mrs. Dewitt.

*

1. Hear the pennies dropping, Listen while they fall,—Every one for
2. Now, while we are lit - tle, Pen-nies are our store; But when we are

Je - sus, He will get them all. Dropping, dropping ev - er,
old - er, Lord, we'll give thee more. Tho' we have not mon - ey,

From each lit - tle hand: 'Tis our gift to Je - sus From His little band.
We can give Him love. He will own our offering, Smiling from above.

J. R. MURRAY.

1. We are little students, Seeking in our youth, Seeking in our youth, Seeking in our

youth, Paths of wisdom, safety, Life, the light, the truth, Life, the light, the truth.

2 Little thoughts and actions,
   ‖: Heed we will with care; :‖
Truth with its attractions
   ‖: Keeps from every snare. :‖

3 Little truths we're learning,
   ‖: On the Sabbath day, :‖
Make us very strong in
   ‖: Virtue's happy way, :‖

4 Little pray'rs ascending,
   ‖: Thro' the sinner's Friend, :‖
Bring returning blessing—
   ‖: Fit us for life's end. :‖

5 Little songs of praises,
   ‖: Lord, we'll raise to Thee, :‖
And in heav'n Thy glories
   ‖: Sing eternally. :‖

I WILL NOT SWEAR. (Infant Class.)

From "Little Sower."   J. R. MURRAY.

1. I will not swear, I will not dare, God's name in vain to take;
2. I will not steal, For I should feel De - grad-ed and a' - shamed;

I will not lie, But I will try, The truth my guide to make.
I will be kind, My parents mind, Nor be a fight - er named.

3 If I begin In youth to sin,
   My misery is sure;
No peace of mind Can I thus find,
   No pleasure good and pure.

4 But if I love Our God above,
   Dear friends and parents kind,
My teachers true, And schoolmates, too,
   Great peace then I shall find.

WE ARE BUT LITTLE CHILDREN WEAK.

C. E. WILLING.

1. We are but lit-tle children weak, Nor born in a-ny high es-tate:

What can we do for Je-sus' sake Who is so high and good and great? Amen.

2 O, day by day each Christian child
  Has much to do, without, within;
  A death to die for Jesus' sake,
  A weary war to wage with sin.

3 When deep within our swelling hearts
  The thoughts of pride and anger rise,
  When bitter words are on our tongues,
  And tears of passion in our eyes;

4 Then we may stay the angry blow,
  Then we may check the hasty word,
  Give gentle answers back again,
  And fight a battle for our Lord.

5 There's not a child so small and weak
  But has his little cross to take,
  His little work of love and praise
  That he may do for Jesus' sake. Amen.

WHO LOVES THE LITTLE CHILDREN?

Words and Music by H. E. KIMBALL.

1. Who loves the little children? Who folds them to His breast? Who, thro' the hours of
2. Who 'mid life's care and turmoil, In sunshine and in storm, In conflict and in
3. Who at the dy-ing pillow, When vain is earthly aid, In gentle accents

CHORUS faster.

dark - ness   Watch - es   their rest?
dan - ger,   Shields from all harm?   'T is Je - sus, our Sav - ior, Re -
whis - pers   Be   not   a - fraid?

deem-er and Friend, His love will sup-ply   all our wants till life's end.

Used by permission of BRAINARD SONS.

MATTIE PEARSON SMITH. S. W. STRAUB.

1. In the morn-ing ear - ly, When the dew is bright,
2. In the fer - vid noon - tide, When the sun is high;
3. In the pur - ple twi - light, When the day is done,

When the flow'rs are smil - ing In the bless - ed light;
When the flocks are seek - ing, Where the shad - ows lie;
And be - hind the hill - tops, Sink - eth low the sun;

When the hap - py song - birds, Thank - ful hom - age pay;
When the brooks are run - ning Dream - ing - ly a - way;
When you pause to rest you, Wea - ry of your play;

To the God who keeps you, Lit - tle chil - dren, pray.
Then to God who sees you, Lit - tle chil - dren, pray.
At that pleas-ant sea - son, Lit - tle chil - dren, pray.

4 When the night is setting
O'er the trackless world,
And the darksome shadows
All the earth enfold;
When the winds are sighing
'Neath the starry way,
Unto God, who keeps you,
Little children, pray.

5 Yes, in times of trouble,
Or in sunny hours;
Whether in the desert,
Or amid the flow'rs,
In the midnight dreary,
Or in times of play;
Unto God, who keeps you,
Little children, pray.

GROWING UP FOR JESUS. (Infant Class.)

P. J. OWENS.   W. J. KIRKPATRICK.

1. Grow-ing up for Je-sus, We are tru-ly blest; In His smile is welcome

In His arms our rest. In His truth our treasure, In His love our rule;

CHORUS.

Growing up for Je-sus, In our Sunday school. Growing up for Jesus,

Till in Him complete; Growing up for Je-sus; Oh, His work is sweet;

Growing up for Jesus, Till in Him complete; Growing up for Jesus; Oh, His work is sweet!

2 Not too young to love Him,
  Little hearts beat true;
Not too young to serve Him
  As the dew-drops do.
Not too young to praise Him,
  Singing as we come;
Not too young to answer
  When He calls us home.

3 Growing up for Jesus,
  Learning day by day
How to follow onward
  In the narrow way.
Seeking holy treasure,
  Finding precious truth;
Growing up for Jesus
  In our happy youth.

JESUS' LITTLE LAMB AM I. (Infant Class.)

ADAM GEIBEL.

1. Je - sus' lit - tle lamb am I, On His goodness I re - ly;

He, my gentle Shepherd, leads me, In His pastures green He feeds me;

For He loves me, knows me well, And my lit - tle name can tell.

2 Underneath His gracious staff
  I go in and out and have
Pasture sweet around me lying,
Still my hungry soul supplying;
When I thirst, my feet He brings
Where the living water springs.

3 Should a lambkin, then, like me,
  Ever sad and thankless be?
When these pleasant days are ended,
On my Shepherd's bosom tended,
I shall go to perfect bliss;
No hope nor joy can equal this.

JESUS LOVES ME SO. (Infant Class.)

MATTIE PEARSON SMITH.   J. W. PRATT. By per.

1. Tho' I am a lit - tle child, Wand'ring thro' a world of woe,

Yet, I have one pre-cious Friend, And He loves me so;

And I will not be afraid, When life's storm-winds fiercely blow;

He is strong, His arm will save, For He loves me so.

2 In the darkest, blackest night,
   I will never be afraid:
He will be close by my side
   Through the dreadful shade;
He will whisper sweetest words,
   Yes, He'll comfort me, I know;
Nothing, then, can hurt me there,
   For He loves me so.

3 Jesus loves me all the time,
   When I'm good, when naughty, too;
When I love Him, or forget,
   He is always true;

Once He died to save my soul,
   Died in agony and woe;
Oh, how can I grieve His heart
   When He loves me so?

4 He will love me evermore;
   Oh, how much to Him I owe!
All that He has done for me,
   I can never know;
Lo, at last when I shall sleep
   In the arms of death so low,
Safely He my soul will keep,
   For He loves me so.

MARGARETTE SNODGRASS.　　　　　　　　T. MARTIN TOWNE. By per.

1. Sing, oh, sing, Lit - tle ones sing; Prais - es bring Un - to the King,
2. Glad - ly beat, Lit-tle hearts beat; Love so sweet, Lay at His feet,
3. Up and do, Lit-tle hearts, true; Days are few, E - ven for you,

Prais-es bring, Un - to the King, Un-to the King of glo - ry!
Love so sweet, Lay at His feet, Happy hearts full of treas-ure.
Days are few, E - ven for you; Up and be ev - er do - ing.

CHORUS.

Un - to the King of glo - ry Loud let the glad notes ring, let them ring;

Un - to the King of glo - ry Loud let the glad notes ring.

8

I AM LITTLE.

J. E. H.

J. E. HALL.

1. I am lit - tle, but I love, I love Je - sus, He loves me;
2. I am lit - tle, but I sing, Sing of Him who came to save;
3. I am lit - tle, but I pray; Je - sus list - ens, He is nigh;
4. I am lit - tle, but I hope Up in heav'n at last to dwell;

I am lit - tle, but I love Near His precious side to be.
I am lit - tle, but I sing, Now His par-don I may have.
I am lit - tle, but I pray, And He hears my hum - ble cry.
I am lit - tle, but I hope, There for aye His praise to tell.

CHORUS.

I am lit - tle, Je - sus knows, For He sees me ev - 'ry day;

I am lit - tle, Je - sus knows, So He leads me all the way.

M. E. Servoss.   Geo. C. Hugg.

With feeling.

1. Waiting for Je-sus, and working while I wait; His lab'rers they are
2. Waiting for Je-sus, and working while I wait; Sow-ing on hill and
3. Waiting for Je-sus, and working while I wait; What tho' the hours seem

few, they are few; So I will work with an earnest, loving heart, And
plain, hill and plain; Reaping with care all the fruit of earnest toil, A
long, hours seem long; Greater the har-vest I then may gar-ner in, And

CHORUS.

hands that are kind and true.
har - vest of gold - en grain.   Wait-ing for Je - sus, and
sweet - er the har - vest - song.

working while I wait; Surely my heart is blest; Waiting for Je-sus, and

work - ing while I wait, And then go - ing home to rest.

LET US SPEAK WELL OF OUR BROTHER.

S. J. VAIL

1. Oh, be not the first to dis-cov-er . . A blot on the fame of a
2. How often the light smile of gladness . Is worn by the friends that we
3. How often the friends we hold dearest . Their noblest e-mo-tions con-

friend, A flaw in the faith of anoth-er, Whose heart may prove true to the end.
meet, To cover a soul full of sadness, Too proud to acknowledge defeat.
ceal; And bosoms the purest, sincerest, Have secrets they can not reveal.

A smile or a sigh may a-wak-en Sus-pi-cion most false and undue;
How oft-en the sigh of de-jec-tion Is heaved from the hypocrite's breast,
We none of us know one anoth-er, And oft in-to er-ror may fall;

And thus our be-lief may be shak-en In hearts that are honest and true.
To par-o-dy truth and af-fec-tion, Or lull a sus-pi-cion to rest.
Then let us speak well of our broth-er, Or speak not about him at all.

CHORUS.

We none of us know one an-oth-er, And oft in-to er-ror may fail;

Then let us speak well of our brother, Or speak not about him at all.

COME AND WELCOME.

F. L. ARMSTRONG.

Firmly.

1. From the cross up - lift - ed high, Where the Sav-ior deigns to die,
2. Sprinkled now with blood the throne, Why be-neath thy bur-dens groan?
3. Spread for thee the fes - tal board, See with rich-est dain -ties stored;

What mel - o - dious sounds I hear, Eurst-ing on my rav-ished ear!
On my pierc - ed bod - y laid, Jus - tice owns the ran - som paid.
To thy Fa - ther's bo - som press'd, Yet a - gain a child con - fessed,

Love's re-deem - ing work is done, Come and welcome, sin - ner, come.
Bow the knee, and kiss the Son, Come and welcome, sin - ner, come.
Nev - er from His house to roam, Come and welcome, sin - ner, come.

Love's re-deem - ing work is done, Come and welcome, sin - ner, come.
Bow the knee and kiss the Son, Come and welcome, sin - ner, come.
Nev - er from His house to roam, Come and welcome, sin - ner, come.

M. E. Servoss.   Adam Geibel.

1. Re-joice! re-joice! for Je - sus reigns, The Prince of peace and love,
2. Re-joice! re-joice! the Christ has come, The Sav - ior of man-kind,
3. Re-joice! re-joice for ev - er - more, Nor let one soul re - pine,

To guide the chil - dren of His grace To heav'n, their home a - bove.
To seek the lost ones of His fold, And heal the halt and blind.
Tho' friends forget, and hearts grow cold, A Fa-ther's love is thine.

And they who seek His lov - ing care Thro' dark and sun - ny days,
Oh, err - ing and re - pent - ant soul, Look up, and thou shalt live;
And if the world seem dark with frowns, Just meet them with a smile;

Shall know how safe - ly they may walk When God di-rects their ways.
The Friend of sin - ners comes to save, To ran - som and for-give.
And, with the hope of fut - ure bliss, All pres - ent ills be-guile.

CHORUS.

Re - joice! re-joice for ev - er-more, Im-man - uel's prais-es sing;

ice who sure - ly know That Je - sus is their King.

LOVE DIVINE.

JOHN ZUNDEL, by per.

all love ex - cel-ling, Joy of heav'n, to earth come down!
athe Thy loving Spirit In - to ev - 'ry troubled breast!
Thy new cre - a - tion, Pure and spotless may we be;

hy hum - ble dwelling, All thy faithful mer-cies crown.
n Thee in-her - it, Let us find Thy prom-ised rest.
ur whole sal-va - tion Per-fect-ly se - cured by Thee.

art all compas-sion, Pure, un-bounded love Thou art;
y to de-liv - er, Let us all Thy grace re - ceive!
ory in - to glo-ry, Till in heav'n we take our place;

ith Thy sal - va-tion, En - ter ev - 'ry trembling heart.
e - turn and nev-er, Nev - er-more Thy tem-ples leave.
ur crowns before Thee, Lost in won-der, love, and praise.

GLORY TO THE FATHER GIVE.

HULLAH.

1. Glo - ry to the Fa - ther give, God in whom we move and live;
2. Glo - ry to the Ho - ly Ghost, He re-claims the sin - ner lost;

Children's prayers He deigns to hear, Children's songs de-light His ear.
Children's minds may He in - spire, Touch their tongues with holy fire.

Glo - ry to the Son we bring, Christ our Prophet, Priest, and King;
Glo - ry in the high - est be To the bless - ed Trin - i - ty,

Rall.

Children, raise your sweetest strain To the Lamb, for He was slain.
For the Gospel from a-bove, For the word that "God is love." A - men.

1 SONS of Zion, raise your songs,
Praise to Zion's King belongs;
His the victor's crown and fame,
Glory to the Savior's name.
Sore the strife, but rich the prize,
Precious in the Victor's eyes;
Glorious is the work achieved,
Satan vanquished, man relieved.

2 Sing we then the Victor's praise,
Go ye forth and strew the ways;
Bid Him welcome to His throne,
He is worthy, He alone.
Place the crown upon His brow;
Every knee to Him shall bow;
Him the brightest seraph sings,
Heaven proclaims Him "King of kings."

T. KELLY.

R. W. RAYMOND.   F. SILCHER.

1. Far out on the des-o-late bil-low, The sail-or sails the sea,
2. Far down in the earth's dark bo-som, The min-er mines the ore;
3. Lord, grant as we sail life's o-cean, Or delve in its mines of woe;

A - lone with the night and the tempest, Where countless dangers be.
Death lurks in the dark be-hind him, And hides in the rock be-fore.
Or fight in its ter-ri-ble conflict, This com-fort all to know:

CHORUS.

Yet nev-er a-lone is the Christian, Who lives by faith and prayer;
Yet nev-er a-lone, etc.
That nev-er a-lone, etc.

For God is a friend un-fail-ing, And God is ev-'ry-where.

THE SWEETEST STORY.

MARY B. SLEIGHT.   REV. E. P. PARKER.

1. There is no sweet-er sto-ry told, In all the Bless-ed Book,

Than how the Lord within His arms, The lit-tle children took.

For their young eyes His sorrowing face A smile of glad-ness wore,—

A smile that for His lit-tle ones, It wear-eth ev-er-more.

2 The voice that silenced priest and scribe,
For them grew low and sweet,
And still for them His gentle lips
The loving words repeat:
"Forbid them not!" O blessed Christ,
We bring them unto Thee,
And pray that on their heads may rest
Thy benedicite.

M. E. SERVOSS.   JNO. R. SWENEY.

1. We will sweetly sing on the golden shore, Where all is joy and glad-ness;
2. We are sure our Father knows all our need, Each heartache, pain, and sorrow;

For ev-er-more with Christ we'll reign, Released from care and sadness.
So in His hands we'll leave it all, And trust Him for the mor-row.

CHORUS.

Then along the way, the Lord's highway, With voices clear and ringing,

We'll shout ho-san-na as we go, And en-ter Zi-on sing-ing.

3 We will sing of Jesus, our Savior-King,
   Whose wondrous love is o'er us;
   Who guides our footsteps, lest they stray,
   And makes all plain before us.

4 We will sing of heaven,—our home above,
   With all its joy and glory;
   And to the world, where'er we go,
   We'll tell salvation's story.

DO IT TO-DAY.

O. D. SHERMAN.   J. M. STILLMAN, by per.

1. If we on - ly knew what good we could do, In this
2. An - y cheer - ing word in gloom that is heard By a
3. And a lov - ing smile, some heart may in-cline To the

world of sin and sor - row, We would not de - lay, but
heart that grief would bor - row, May light - en the load, and
path that's straight and nar - row; A kind, friend-ly deed to

do it to-day, And nev - er wait for to - mor - row, No,
bright-en the road, So nev - er wait for to - mor - row, No,
one in his need Is bet - ter now than to - mor - row, Yes,

nev - er wait for to - mor-row, No, nev - er wait for to-mor-row, But
nev - er wait for to - mor-row, No, nev - er wait for to-mor-row, But
bet - ter now than to - mor-row, Yes, bet - ter now than to-mor-row, So

do it to-day, and nev - er de-lay, And save a world of sor - row.
speak it to-day, and nev - er de-lay, 'Twill lift the clouds of sor - row.
do it to-day, and nev - er de-lay, And save a world of sor - row.

JAMES EDMESTON.

1. Lit-tle travel-ers Zi-on-ward, Each one enter-ing in-to rest,

In the king-dom of your Lord, In the man-sions of the blest.

There, to wel-come, Je-sus waits, Gives the crowns His followers win;

Lift your heads, ye gold-en gates, Let the lit-tle travelers in.

2 Who are they whose little feet,
  Pacing life's dark journey through,
Now have reached that heavenly seat
  They had ever kept in view?
"I from Greenland's frozen land;"
  "I from India's sultry plain;"
"I from Afric's barren sand;"
  "I from islands of the main."

3 All our earthly journey past,
  Every tear and pain gone by,
Here together met at last,
  At the portal of the sky:
Each the welcome, "Come," awaits
  Conquerors over death and sin;
Lift your heads, ye golden gates,
  Let the little travelers in.

TENDER SHEPHERD, THOU HAST STILLED.

Miss C. Winkworth, tr.

Arthur S. Sullivan.

1. Ten - der Shep - herd, Thou hast stilled Now Thy lit - tle

lamb's brief weep - ing; Ah, how peace - ful, pale, and mild

In its nar - row bed 'tis sleep - ing! And no sigh of

an - guish sore Heaves that lit - tle bo - som more.

2 In this world of care and pain,
   Lord, Thou wouldst no longer leave it;
To the sunny heavenly plain
   Thou dost now with joy receive it;
Clothed in robes of spotless white,
Now it dwells with Thee in light.

3 Ah, Lord Jesus, grant that we
   Where it lives may soon be living,
And the lovely pastures see
   That its heavenly food are giving;
Then the gain of death we prove,
Though Thou take what most we love.

D. NELSON. GEORGE F. ROOT.

1. My days are glid - ing swift-ly by, And I, a pil-grim stran-ger,
2. We'll gird our loins, my brethren dear, Our heavenly home dis-cern - ing;

Would not de-tain them as they fly, Those hours of toil and dan-ger.
Our ab - sent Lord has left us word, "Let ev - 'ry lamp be burn-ing."

CHORUS.

For oh, we stand on Jordan's strand, Our friends are pass-ing o - ver;

And just be-fore, the shining shore We may al-most dis - cov-er.

3 Should coming days be cold and
    dark,
We need not cease our singing;
That perfect rest nought can molest,
Where golden harps are ringing.

4 Let sorrow's rudest tempest blow,
    Each cord on earth to sever;
Our King says, "Come!" and there's
    our home,
    Forever, oh, forever.

IN THE CROSS OF CHRIST I GLORY.

BROWNING.   CONKEY.

1. In the cross of Christ I glo-ry, Tow-'ring o'er the wrecks of time;

All the light of sa - cred sto-ry Gathers round its head sublime.

2 When the woes of life o'ertake me,
    Hopes deceive and fears annoy,
  Never shall the cross forsake me:
    Lo! it glows with peace and joy.

3 When the sun of bliss is beaming
    Light and love upon my way,
  From the cross the radiance streaming,
    Adds new luster to the day.

4 Bane and blessing, pain and pleasure,
    By the cross are sanctified;
  Peace is there, that knows no measure,
    Joys that through all time abide.

5 In the cross of Christ I glory,
    Tow'ring o'er the wrecks of time;
  All the light of sacred story
    Gathers round its head sublime.

1 Sweet the moments, rich in blessing,
    Which before the cross I spend;
  Life, and health, and peace possessing,
    From the sinner's dying Friend.

2 Truly blessed is my station,
    Low before His cross to lie;
  While I see divine compassion
    Floating in His languid eye.

3 Here it is I find my heaven
    While upon the cross I gaze;
  Love I much? I've much forgiven,
    I'm a miracle of grace.

4 Love and grief my heart dividing,
    With my tears His feet I'll bathe;
  Constant still in faith abiding,
    Life deriving from His death,
                          ALLEN.

Arr. by LOWELL MASON.

ny God, to Thee, Near - er   to Thee: E'en though it
the wand-er - er, The   sun   gone down,   Dark - ness be
he way   ap-pear Steps   un - to heaven;   All that Thou

ss That rais - eth me;   Still   all   my song shall be,
, My   rest   a stone;   Yet   in   my dreams I'd be
, In   mer - cy given;   An - gels to beck - on me

God, to Thee, Nearer, my God, to Thee, Near - er to Thee.
God, to Thee, Nearer, my God, to Thee, Near - er to Thee.
God, to Thee, Nearer, my God, to Thee, Near - er to Thee.

aking thoughts
ny praise,
griefs
e;
o be
d, to Thee,
to Thee,
e.

ring
ty,
tars forgot,

shall be,
d, to Thee,
to Thee,
e.

1 Fade, fade, each earthly joy;
    Jesus is mine.
Break, every tender tie;
    Jesus is mine.
Dark is the wilderness,
Earth has no resting-place,
Jesus alone can bless;
    Jesus is mine.

2 Tempt not my soul away;
    Jesus is mine.
Here would I ever stay;
    Jesus is mine.
Perishing things of clay,
Born but for one brief day,
Pass from my heart away;
    Jesus is mine.
             H. BONAR.

CORONATION. C. M.

E. PERRONET.　　　　　　　　　　　　　　　　　　　　　OLIVER HOLDEN.

1. All hail the power of Je - sus' name! Let an - gels prostrate fall,

Bring forth the roy - al di - a - dem, And crown Him Lord of all;

Bring forth the roy-al di - a - dem, And crown Him Lord of all.

2 Crown Him, ye morning stars of light,
　Who fixed this floating ball;
Now hail the strength of Israel's might,
　And crown Him Lord of all.

3 Crown Him, ye martyrs of your God,
　Who from His altar call;
Extol the stem of Jesse's rod,
　And crown Him Lord of all.

4 Ye seed of Israel's chosen race,
　Ye ransomed of the fall,
Hail Him, who saves you by His grace,
　And crown Him Lord of all.

5 Let every kindred, every tribe,
　On this terrestrial ball,
To Him all majesty ascribe,
　And crown Him Lord of all.

MARTYN. 7s. Double.

C. WESLEY.　　　　　　　　　　　　　　　　　　　　　S. B. MARSH.
　　　　　　　　　　　　　　　　　　　　　　　　　　　Fine.

Je - sus, lov-er of my soul, Let me to Thy bo - som fly,
While the billows near me roll, While the tempest still is high:
D.C. Safe in - to the ha - ven guide, Oh, re - ceive my soul at last.

Hide me, oh, my Sav - ior, hide, Till the storm of life is past;

C. WESLEY. J. P. HOLBROOK. By per.

DUET. Alto and Bass.

1. Je-sus, lov-er of my soul, Let me to Thy bo-som fly,

While the bil - lows near me roll, While the tem - pest still is high:

CHORUS.

Hide me, oh, my Sav-ior, hide, Till the storm of life is past;

Safe in-to the ha-ven guide; Oh, re-ceive my soul at last.

2 Other refuge have I none;
  Hangs my helpless soul on Thee:
Leave, ah! leave me not alone,
  Still support and comfort me:
All my trust on Thee is stayed,
  All my help from Thee I bring;
Cover my defenseless head
  With the shadow of Thy wing.

3 Thou, O Christ, art all I want,
  More than all in Thee I find:
Raise the fallen, cheer the faint,
  Heal the sick, and lead the blind:

Just and holy is Thy name;
  I am all unrighteousness:
False and full of sin I am;
  Thou art full of truth and grace.

4 Plenteous grace with Thee is found,
  Grace to cover all my sin;
Let the healing streams abound,
  Make and keep me pure within:
Thou of life the fountain art,
  Freely let me take of Thee;
Spring Thou up within my heart;
  Rise to all eternity.

S. S. Hymnal, by per.

1. All praise to Thee, our Fa - ther, For Thy re-deem-ing grace;

All praise to Thee, O Je - sus, The Sav - ior of our race.

Dear Je - sus, low be-fore Thee, We bend in fear and love;

Oh, grant we may a - dore Thee, In Thy bright realms a - bove.

2 Pure as the light of heaven,
  In meekness most divine;
Such grace to us be given,
  Dear Savior, as was Thine.
Thy precious cross and passion
  Did for our sins atone;
Oh, grant us Thy forgiveness,
  And make us all Thine own.

3 If any have forsaken
  Thy ways, by willful sin,
Oh, let them now be taken
  Back to Thy fold again.
Oh, shed abroad within us
  The Spirit of Thy grace;
In mercy, Lord, oh, bring us
  To see Thy lovely face.

S. S. Hymnal, by per.

1. For the beau-ty of the earth, For the glo-ry
2. For the won-der of each hour, Of the day and

of the skies, For the love which from our birth
of the night; Hill and vale, and tree, and flower,

CHORUS.

O-ver and a-round us lies; Lord of all, to
Sun and moon, and stars of light; Lord of all, to

Thee we raise, This our grate-ful psalm of praise.
Thee we raise, This our grate-ful psalm of praise.

3 For the joy of human love,
   Brother, sister, parent, child;
  Friends on earth, and friends above,
   Pleasures pure and undefiled;
  Lord of all, to Thee we raise
  This our grateful psalm of praise.

4 For Thy church that evermore
   Lifts her holy hands above,
  Offering up on every shore
   Her pure sacrifice of love ;
  Lord of all, to Thee we raise
  This our grateful psalm of praise.

SCHMOLKE.   WEBER.

1. My Je - sus, as Thou wilt! Oh! may Thy will be mine; In - to Thy hand of love I would my all re - sign; Through sorrow, or through joy, Conduct me as thine own, And help me still to say, My Lord, Thy will be done!

1 My Jesus, as thou wilt!
  Oh! may Thy will be mine;
Into Thy hand of love
  I would my all resign;
Through sorrow, or through joy,
  Conduct me as Thine own,
And help me still to say,
  My Lord, Thy will be done.

2 My Jesus, as Thou wilt!
  Though seen through many a tear,
Let not my star of hope
  Grow dim or disappear:
Since Thou on earth hast wept,
  And sorrowed oft alone,
If I must weep with Thee,
  My Lord, Thy will be done!

3 My Jesus, as Thou wilt!
  All shall be well for me;
Each changing future scene
  I gladly trust with Thee:
Straight to my home above
  I travel calmly on,
And sing, in life or death,
  My Lord, Thy will be done!

1 Thy way, not mine, O Lord,
  However dark it be!
Lead me by Thine own hand;
  Choose out the path for me.
I dare not choose my lot:
  I would not, if I might;
Choose Thou for me, my God,
  So shall I walk aright.

2 The kingdom that I seek
  Is Thine: so let the way
That leads to it be Thine,
  Else I must surely stray.
Take Thou my cup, and it
  With joy or sorrow fill,
As best to Thee may seem;
  Choose Thou my good and ill.

3 Choose Thou for me my friends,
  My sickness or my health;
Choose Thou my cares for me,
  My poverty or wealth.
Not mine, not mine the choice,
  In things or great or small.
Be Thou my Guide, my Strength,
  My Wisdom, and my All.

                       BONAR.

MY COUNTRY, 'TIS OF THEE.

S. F. SMITH.

1. My country 'tis of thee, Sweet land of lib-er-ty, Of thee I sing; Land where my
2. My native country, thee, Land of the noble, free, Thy name I love; I love thy
3. Our fathers' God, to thee, Author of lib-er-ty, To thee we sing; Long may our

fathers died, Land of the pilgrim's pride, From ev'ry mountain side Let freedom ring.
rocks and rills, Thy woods and templed hills; My heart with rapture thrills Like that a-bove.
land be bright With freedom's holy light; Protect us by Thy might, Great, God our King.

GOD BLESS OUR NATIVE LAND.

J. S. DWIGHT. (A.)

1. God bless our native land: Firm may she ever stand, Thro' storm and night,
2. For her our pray'r shall rise To God, above the skies; On Him we wait,

Through storm and night; When the wild tempests rave, Ru - ler of
On Him we wait; Thou who art ev - er nigh, Guard-ing with

wind and wave, Do Thou our country save By Thy great might.
watch-ful eye, To Thee a - loud we cry, God save the State.

SHOUT WE WITH JOY.

WM. C. DALAND.
WM. C. DALAND.

f Allegro.

1. Shout! shout a-loud! a free, gladsome throng, Once more we come with
2. Heavenward we journey; Lord, 'tis from Thee Comes all our help and
3. Let once a-gain our glad voic-es ring An-thems of praise to

bright, hap-py song, Chanting in notes of praise to pro-long
guid-ance so free; Keep us, though proud and wayward are we,
Je - sus, our King; 'Tis of His wondrous love that we sing

This our joy-ous lay. Thanks to our great Cre - a - tor we owe,
Ev - er in Thy love. Now in our hearts do Thou e'er re-main;
As we now a - dore. And when on high our Sav - ior we greet,

mf   Cres.

For all the bless-ings He doth be-stow; And we our grat - i-
All oth-er trust is nought but in vain; Oh, take us with Thee,
When we our crowns shall lay at His feet, Then we a - new our

Rit. f

tude e'er will show On this fes - tal day.
when Thou shalt reign On Thy throne a - bove.
song will re - peat— Praise for ev - er - more.

CHORUS. ff A Tempo.

Then shout we with joy our prais - es to Thee, Lord, whom we hail with
Then shout we with joy our prais - es to Thee, Lord, whom we hail with
Then shout we with joy our prais - es to Thee, Lord, whom we hail with

hearts light and free! On this our day of
hearts light and free! On this our day of
hearts light and free! On this our day of

Rit.

glad ju - bi - lee, Praise to Thee we pay.
glad ju - bi - lee, Praise we for Thy love.
glad, ju - bi - lee, Praise we ev - er - more.

HENRY SMART.

1. Heavenly Father, send Thy bless-ing On Thy children gathered here;
2. Bear Thy lambs when they are weary, In Thine arms, and at Thy breast;

May they all, Thy name con-fess - ing, Be to Thee for - ev - er dear.
Thro' life's desert, dry and drear - y, Bring them to Thy heavenly rest.

Ho - ly Sav-ior, who in meek-ness Didst vouchsafe a Child to be;
Spread Thy golden pinions o'er them, Ho - ly Spir - it, from a - bove;

Guide their steps, and help their weakness, Bless and make them like to Thee.
Guide them, lead them, go before them, Give them peace, and joy, and love. Amen.

Rev. John Mason Neale, tr.

J. P. Holbrook.

1. Art thou wea - ry, art thou lan - guid, Art thou sore dis-tressed?

"Come to me," saith One, "and com - ing Be at rest."

Copyright, 1882, by J. P. Holbrook.

2 Hath He marks to lead me to Him,
  If He be my Guide?
"In His feet and hands are wound-prints,
  And His side."

3 Is there diadem as Monarch,
  That His brow adorns?
"Yea, a crown in very surety,
  But of thorns!"

4 If I still hold closely to Him,
  What hath He at last?
"Sorrow vanquished, labor ended,
  Jordan past!"

5 If I ask Him to receive me,
  Will He say me nay?
"Not till earth, and not till heaven
  Pass away!"

1. Art thou wea - ry, art thou lan - guid, Art thou sore dis-tressed?

"Come to me," saith One, "and com - ing Be at rest."

HUSHED WAS THE EVENING HYMN.

A. SULLIVAN.

1. Hushed was the evening hymn, The tem - ple courts were dark,
2. Oh! give me Sam - uel's ear, The o - pen ear, O Lord,

The lamp was burn - ing dim Be - fore the sa - cred ark:
A - live and quick to hear Each whis - per of Thy word;

When sud-den-ly a voice di-vine Rang thro' the silence of the shrine.
Like him to answer at Thy call, And to o - bey Thee first of all.

3 Oh! give me Samuel's heart,
   A lowly heart, that waits
Where in Thy House Thou art,
   Or watches at Thy gates.
By day and night, a heart that still
Moves at the breathing of Thy will.

4 Oh! give me Samuel's mind,
   A sweet, unmurmuring faith,
Obedient and resigned
   To Thee in life and death,
That I may read with childlike eyes
Truths that are hidden from the wise.

O. D. Sherman. J. M. Stillman.

Allegretto.

1. There is a beau-ty born of love, More bright than sunshine beaming,
2. That beau-ty beams from Zion's mount, And glows in Bethle'm's story,

More radiant than the stars a-bove, Or gold and diamonds gleaming.
Il-lumes Sa-ma-ria's sacred fount, And makes the Cross our glory.

CHORUS.

Oh, beau-ty, bright and fair, di-vine, The world has known thee never;

Oh, may thy light a-round me shine, And guide my way for-ev-er.

3 That beauty crowns the lowly saint,
  Whose heart its light is cheering,
Who, toiling on, shall never faint,
  But wait the Lord's appearing.

4 And when the light of life grows dim,
  And fades all earthly pleasure,
The beauty of the Lord shall win
  An everlasting treasure.

By permission of Stillman & Towne.

IT PAYS TO DO RIGHT.

F. S. POND.

T. MARTIN TOWNE, by per.

Not too slow.

1. Tho' temptation, the envoy of wrath, Paint the future with beauty and gold,
2. Happy we if our conscience may rest From the demon of sin ev-er free,
3. Oh, it pays to be noble and true, Tho' the world may condemn and despise,

And the roses e'er streweth our path, Luring onward to "treasures untold;"
While the beautiful home of the blest Waiteth yonder for you and for me;
For the mercy of God, like the dew, Falleth gently on whom it de-cries;

'Neath the roses lurk sorrow and gloom, And the path leads to ruin and night,
Then we have our reward even here, If we walk in the truth and its might,
Let us cling closely, then, to the cross, Thro' the darkness no less than the light,

While the future brings sentence of doom Unto him who stood not for the right.
While the Shepherd of souls standeth near, Guarding us when we dare to do right.
And account all the world but as dross, If it weigh with the wrong 'gainst the right.

CHORUS. (*For last verse repeat Chorus ppp.*).........

Oh, it pays .... to do right, ... Oh, it

Oh, it pays to do right, Oh, it pays to do right,

pays . . to do right, . . .

pays, it pays to do right, to do right; Let us walk in the truth, in the

Rit.

truth and the light, For it pays, yes, it pays, to do right, to do right.

OH, BLESSED IS THAT LAND.

CHATTERTON DIX. Arranged from DR. STAINER, by REV. E. P. PARKER.

Oh, bless-ed is that land of God, Where saints a-bide for - ev - er,

Where golden fields spread far and broad, Where flows the crystal riv-er; Oh,

Cres.

blessed! thrice blessed, the strains of all its holy throng, With ours below are

blending; Thrice blessed is that heav'nly song, Which never hath an ending;

Thrice bless-ed is that heav'nly song, Which nev-er hath an end-ing;

P Rall. *PP Rall.*

Which nev-er hath an end-ing, Which never hath an end-ing. A - men.

E. S. CARTER.

1. Day by day we mag - ni-fy Thee—When our hymns in school we raise;

Dai-ly work be-gun and ended, With the dai - ly voice of praise. A-men.

2 Day by day we magnify Thee—
  When, as each new day is born,
  On our knees at home we bless Thee
  For the mercies of the morn.

3 Day by day we magnify Thee—
  In our hymns before we sleep;
  Angels hear them, watching by us,
  Christ's dear Lambs all night to keep.

4 Day by day we magnify Thee—
  Not in words of praise alone;
  Truthful lips and meek obedience
  Show Thy glory in Thine own.

5 Then on that eternal morning,
  With Thy great redeeméd host,
  May we fully magnify Thee—
  Father, Son, and Holy Ghost! Amen.

JESUS, HIGH IN GLORY.

T. R. MATTHEWS.

1. Je - sus, high in glo - ry, Lend a listen - ing ear,
2. Tho' Thou art so ho - ly, Heav'n's Al - might - y King,
3. Save us, Lord, from sin - ning, Watch us day by day;
4. Then when Je - sus calls us To our heav'n-ly home,

When we bow be - fore Thee, Chil-dren's prais - es hear.
Thou wilt stoop to list - en, When Thy praise we sing.
Help us now to love Thee, Take our sins a - way.
We would glad - ly an - swer, Sav - ior, Lord, we come. A - men.

D. A. Thrupp.   C. Steggall.

1. Sav - ior, like a Shepherd lead us, Much we need Thy ten-der care;

In Thy pleasant pas-tures feed us, For our use Thy folds prepare.

Bless-ed Je - sus, Bless-ed Je - sus, Thou hast bought us, Thine we are.

2 We are weak, do Thou befriend us,
  Be the guardian of our way;
Keep Thy flock, from sin defend us,
  Seek us when we go astray.
Blessed Jesus, Blessed Jesus,
  Hear, oh, hear us when we pray.

3 Thou hast promised to receive us,
  Poor and sinful though we be;
Thou hast mercy to relieve us,
  Grace to cleanse, and power to free.
Blessed Jesus, Blessed Jesus,
  Let us early turn to Thee.

4 Early let us seek Thy favor,
  Early let us do Thy will;
Holy Lord, our only Savior,
  With Thy grace our bosoms fill.
Blessed Jesus, Blessed Jesus,
  Thou hast loved us, love us still.

The Better Country.

1 Shepherd of Thine Israel lead us,
  Pilgrims through this desert land;
Thou who hast from bondage freed us,
  Guard us by Thy mighty hand.
Daily feed us, Daily feed us,
  Till we reach the heavenly strand.

2 As Thou didst in wondrous manner
  Guide Thy chosen flock aright,
Let Thy presence be our banner,
  Cloud by day, and fire by night.
Thy protection, Thy protection,
  Be our shield, Thy word our light.

3 When we come to Death's dark river,
  Should we dread the swelling tide,
Death of death, life's Source and Giver,
  Bid the narrow stream divide.
Joyful praises, Joyful praises
  We will sing on Canaan's side.
                          Josiah Conder.

H. F. LYTE.   J. P. HOLBROOK.

1. Je - sus, I my cross have taken, All to leave and fol-low Thee;
2. Man may trouble and dis-tress me, 'Twill but drive me to Thy breast;

Nak - ed, poor, despised, for-sak - en, Thou from hence my all shalt be.
Life with tri-als hard may press me, Heav'n will bring me sweeter rest.

Per - ish ev - 'ry fond am - bi - tion, All I've sought, or hoped, or known,
Oh! 'tis not in grief to harm me, While Thy love is left to me;

Yet how rich is my con - di-tion, God and heav'n are still my own.
Oh! 'twere not in joy to charm me, Were that joy unmixed with Thee.

3 Soul, then know thy full salvation,
  Rise o'er sin, and fear, and care;
Joy to find in every station
  Something still to do or bear.
Think what Spirit dwells within thee;
  Think what Father's smiles are thine;
Think that Jesus died to win thee,
  Child of heaven, canst thou repine?

4 Haste thee on from grace to glory,
  Armed by faith, and winged by prayer;
Heaven's eternal day's before thee,
  God's own hand shall guide thee there.
Soon shall pass thy earthly mission,
  Soon shall close thy pilgrim days,
Hope shall change to glad fruition,
  Faith to sight, and prayer to praise.

SPOHR.

1. I heard the voice of Je-sus say, "Come un-to me and rest;

Lay down, thou wea-ry one, lay down Thy head up-on my breast."

I came to Je-sus as I was, Wea-ry and worn and sad;

I found in Him a rest-ing-place, And He hath made me glad.

2 I heard the voice of Jesus say,
  "Behold, I freely give
The living water, thirsty one,
  Stoop down, and drink and live."
I came to Jesus, and I drank
  Of that life-giving stream;
My thirst was quenched, my soul revived,
  And now I live in Him.

3 I heard the voice of Jesus say,
  "I am this dark world's light:
Look unto Me; thy morn shall rise,
  And all thy day be bright."
I looked to Jesus, and I found
  In Him my Star, my Sun;
And in that life of light I'll walk
  Till all my journey's done.

J. P. H.

1. Je - sus, Thy name I love, All oth - er names a - bove,
2. Thou, bless - ed Son of God, Hast bought me with Thy blood,

Je - sus, my Lord! Oh, Thou art all to me! Noth - ing to
Je - sus, my Lord! Oh, how great is Thy love! All oth - er

please I see, Noth-ing a - part from Thee, Je - sus, my Lord!
loves a - bove, Love that I dai - ly prove, Je - sus, my Lord!

HOW GENTLE GOD'S COMMANDS!

NAEGELI.

1. How gen - tle God's com-mands! How kind His pre - cepts are!
2. While Prov - i - dence sup-ports, Let saints se - cure - ly dwell;
3. Why should this anx - ious load Press down your wea - ry mind?
4. His good - ness stands ap-proved, Down to the pres - ent day;

"Come, cast your bur-dens on the Lord, And trust His constant care."
That hand, which bears all nat - ure up, Shall guide His children well.
Haste to your heavenly Fa-ther's throne, And sweet refreshment find.
I'll drop my bur - den at His feet, And bear a song a - way.

AND CAN IT BE?

REV. CHAS. WESLEY.   ARR. by JER. INGALLS.

1. And can it be that I should gain An int'rest in the Savior's blood?
Died He for me, who caus'd His pain? For me, who Him to death pursued?

A - ma-zing love! how can it be That Thou, my Lord, shouldst die for me?

A - ma-zing love! how can it be That Thou, my Lord, shouldst die for me?

2 'T is myst'ry all, the Immortal dies!
  Who can explore His strange design?
In vain the first-born seraph tries
  To sound the depths of love divine;
'T is mercy all! let earth adore:
Let angel minds inquire no more.

3 He left His Father's throne above;
  (So free, so infinite His grace!)
Emptied Himself of all but love,
  And bled for Adam's helpless race;
'T is mercy all, immense and free,
For O, my God, it found out me!

4 Long my imprisoned spirit lay
  Fast bound in sin and nature's night;
Thine eyes diffused a quick'ning ray:
  I woke; the dungeon flamed with light;
My chain fell off my heart was free—
I rose, went forth and followed Thee.

5 No condemnation now I dread;
  Jesus, with all in Him, is mine;
Alive in Him, my living Head,
  And clothed in righteousness divine,
Bold I approach the eternal throne
And claim the crown thro' Christ my own.

WHEN THROUGH THE TORN SAIL. 151

R. HEBER.   A. S. SULLIVAN.

1. When thro' the torn sail the wild tempest is streaming, When o'er the dark
2. O Jesus, once tossed on the breast of the billow, A-roused by the

wave the red lightning is gleam-ing, Nor hope lends a ray, the poor
shriek of de-spair from Thy pil-low, Now seat-ed in glo-ry, the

sea-man to cher-ish, We fly to our Maker: "Save, Lord, or we perish."
mar-i-ner cher-ish! Who cries, in his anguish, "Save, Lord, or we perish."

STAR OF PEACE.

JANE C. B. SIMPSON.   J. P. HOLBROOK.

1. Star of peace, to wanderers wea-ry, Bright the beams that smile on me;
2. Star of hope, gleam on the billow, Bless the soul that sighs for thee;

Cheer the pilot's vision dreary, Far, far, far at sea, Far, far, far at sea.
Bless the sailor's lonely pillow, Far, far, far at sea, Far, far, far at sea.

3 Star of faith, when winds are mocking
   All his toil, he flies to thee:
Save him on the billows rocking,
   Far, far at sea.

4 Star divine, O safely guide him,
   Bring the wanderer home to thee:
Sore temptations long have tried him,
   Far, far at sea.

E. CASWALL.　　　　　　　　　　　　　　　　　　　　J. B. DYKES.
For verses 1, 2, 3, 5, 6, 7.

1. Days and moments quickly fly - ing, Speed us onward to the dead!

Oh, how soon shall we be ly - ing Each within his nar-row bed!

1 Days and moments quickly flying,
　Speed us onward to the dead!
Oh, how soon shall we be lying
　Each within his narrow bed!

2 Jesus, merciful Redeemer,
　Rouse dead souls to hear Thy voice;
Wake, oh, wake each idle dreamer,
　Now to make th' eternal choice.

3 Mark we whither we are wending;
　Ponder how we soon must go
To inherit bliss unending,
　Or eternity of woe.

4 Life passeth soon: death draweth near:
　Keep us, good Lord, till thou appear;
With Thee to live, with Thee to die,
　With Thee to reign through eternity!

5 As a shadow life is fleeting:
　As a vapor so it flies;
For the old year now retreating
　Pardon grant, and make us wise—

6 Wise that we our days may number,
　Strive and wrestle with our sin,
Stay not in our work, nor slumber
　Till thy glorious rest we win.

7 Soon before the Judge all-glorious,
　We with all the dead shall stand;
Savior, over death victorious,
　Place us then on Thy right hand.

8 Life passeth soon: death draweth near;
　Keep us, good Lord, till Thou appear;
With Thee to live, with Thee to die,
　With Thee to reign through eternity.

For verses 4 and 8.

4. Life passeth soon: death draweth near: Keep us, good Lord, till Thou appear; With Thee to live,

with Thee to die, With Thee to reign thro' eter - - ni-ty. A - men.

Arr. from the German.

Graeioso.

1. The ro-seate hues of ear-ly dawn The brightness of the day, The

crimson of the sun-set sky; How fast they fade a-way, How

fast they fade a-way. Oh, for the pearly gates of heav'n, Oh, for the

golden floor; Oh, for the Sun of Righteousness That setteth nevermore.

2 The highest hopes we cherish here,
  How fast they tire and faint;
How many a spot defiles the robe
  That wraps an earthly saint.
Oh, for a heart that never sins,
  Oh, for a soul washed white;
Oh, for a voice to praise our King,
  Nor weary day or night.

3 Here faith is ours, and heavenly hope,
  And grace to lead us higher;
But there are perfectness and peace
  Beyond our best desire.
Oh, by Thy love and anguish, Lord,
  Oh, by Thy life laid down,
Oh, that we fall not from Thy grace,
  Nor cast away our crown.

CHRISTOPHER WORDSWORTH.   German Melody.

1. Oh, day of rest and glad-ness! Oh, day of joy and light!
2. On thee, at the cre - a - tion, The light first had its birth;

Oh, balm of care and sad - ness! Most beau - ti - ful, most bright;
On thee, for our sal - va - tion, Christ rose from depths of earth;

On thee, the high and low - ly, Through a - ges joined in tune,
On thee, our Lord, vic - to - rious, The Spir - it sent from heaven,

Sing ho - ly, ho - ly, ho - ly, To the great God Tri - une.
And thus on thee, most glo - rious, A tri - ple light was given.

3 To-day on weary nations
  The heavenly manna falls;
To holy convocations
  The silver trumpet calls,
Where gospel light is glowing
  With pure and radiant beams,
And living water flowing,
  With soul-refreshing streams.

4 New graces ever gaining
  From this our day of rest,
We reach the rest remaining
  To spirits of the blest;
To Holy Ghost be praises,
  To Father, and to Son;
The Church her voice upraises
  To Thee, blest Three in One.

TENNYSON.   LINDSAY. Arr. by J. P. HOLBROOK.

SOLO (Soprano or Duet). Vs. 1, 2, 3.

1. Late, late, so late! and dark the night, and chill! Late, late, so late, But we can enter still.

SOLO (Bass).   QUARTET.   End'g for 2d V.   QUARTET.

Too late! too late! ye can not enter now. Too late! too late, ye can not enter now.

2 No light had we;—for that we do repent,
And learning this, the Bridegroom will relent.—
‖: Too late, too late, ye can not enter now. :‖

3 No light! so late! and dark and chill the night—
Oh, let us in, that we may find the light.
‖: Too late, too late, ye can not enter now. :‖

4th Verse.

4. Have we not heard the Bridegroom is so sweet! Oh, let us in, that

DUET.   QUARTET.

we may kiss His feet; Oh, let us in, Oh, let us in, tho' late, to

SOLO (Bass or Contralto). pp QUARTET.

kiss His feet. No! no! too late; ye can not en-ter now!

J. BARNBY.

1. Sleep thy last sleep, Free from care and sorrow; Rest where none weep,

Till the eternal morrow; Tho' dark waves roll O'er the silent riv - er,

Thine upborne soul Is with Je - sus ev - er. A - men.

2 Life's dream is past,
  All its sin and sadness;
Brightly at last
  Dawns a day of gladness.
Dust unto dust;
  Unto God the spirit,
Where, such our trust,
  Life it doth inherit.

3 Though we may mourn
  Those on earth the dearest,
They shall return,
  Christ, when Thou appearest!
Then let Thy voice
  Comfort those now weeping;
They shall rejoice,
  Now in Jesus sleeping.

THY WILL BE DONE.

L. MASON.

"Thy will be | done!" ‖ In devious way
The hurrying stream of | life may | run;‖
Yet still our grateful hearts shall say, ‖
   "Thy will be done."

"Thy will be | done!" ‖ If o'er us shine,
A gladdening and a | prosperous | sun, ‖

This prayer will make it more divine—|
   "Thy will be done."

"Thy will be'done!" ‖ Tho' shrouded o'er
Our ∫ path with | gloom,‖ one comfort—one
Is ours:—to breathe, while we adore, |
   "Thy will be done."

Close by repeating the first two measures—"Thy will be done."

PHEBE CARY.   From "HOLBROOK's Quartet and Chorus Choir."

1. One sweetly solemn thought Comes to me . . | o'er and | o'er:
2. Nearer the bound of life, Where we lay our. . | bur - dens | down;
3. Father, perfect my trust! Strengthen the . . | might of my | faith;

I am nearer home to-day Than I ever . . . have | been be - | fore.
Nearer leaving the cross; Near - - - - - - er | gaining the | crown;
Let me feel as I would When I stand on the rock of the | shore of | death—

Nearer my Father's house, Where the | many mansions | be; | Nearer . the
But lying darkly between, Winding | down through the night, | Is the deep and
Feel as I would when my feet Are | slipping over the brink: | For it may be, I'm

great white | throne, | Nearer the . . | crys - tal | sea.
un - known | stream, | That leads at . | last to the | light.
near - er | home, | Nearer . . . . | now than I | think.

INDEX.

	AUTHOR.	COMPOSER OR SOURCE.	PAGE
Abide with me	H. F. Lyte	W. H. Monk	18
All for God	F. R. Havergal	C. S. H.	11
All glory in the highest	Nat'l Hymn of Holland	S. S. Hymnal.	83
All hail the power of Jesus' name	E. Perronet	O. Holden	130
All is bright and cheerful round us			26
All praise to thee our Father		S. S. Hymnal	132
All this night bright angels sing	Wm. Austin	Sullivan	55
Alleluia fairest morning		R. B. Borthwick	9
And can it be	Ch. Wesley	J. Ingalls	150
Angel voices ever singing	F. Pott	A. S. Sullivan	34
Angry words		H. R. Palmer	28
Art thou weary, art thou languid	J. M. Neale tr.	J. P. Holbrook	139
As Christ upon the cross	E. Caswall	H. Smart	34
Be active	Luther James	T. Martin Towne	101
Be near us	E. P. P.	S. S. Hymnal	86
Beautiful land of rest		"	98
Behold that blood-stained banner	E. E. Rexford	T. Martin Towne	46
Blest be thy love, dear Lord	J. Austin	J. P. H.	88
Brightly gleams our banner	F. J. Potter	Haydn	17
Brighter still and brighter	G. Thring	J. P. Holbrook	35
Christ in the ship	Dean Alford	E. P. Parker	105
Christ was born on Christmas day		Carol	56
Close to thee	F. Crosby	S. J. Vail	47
Come and welcome	F. L. Armstrong	'Crowning Triumph'	117
Come, children, join and sing		Rossini	24
Come, my soul, thou must be waking	F. R. Lewis	J. Stainer	19
Come, oh come, to Jesus		H. C. Camp	75
Come unto me, ye weary	W. C. Dix	J. P. Holbrook	32
Come, ye faithful, raise the strain	J. M. Neale, tr.	A. S. Sullivan	60
Come, ye thankful people, come	Dean Alford	Dr. G. J. Elvey	85
Coronation	E. Perronet	O. Holden	130
Crusaders' hymn		Anon	30
Daily work	E. P. Parker	S. S. Hymnal	77
Day by day we magnify thee		E. S. Carter	145
Days and moments quickly flying	E. Caswall	J. B. Dykes	152
Dear Jesus ever at my side	F. W. Faber	W. H. Havergal	50
Do it day	O. D. Sherman	J. M. Stillman	124
Evening hymn	C. Malan	*	74
Fade, fade each earthly joy	H. Bonar	L. Mason	129
Fairest Lord Jesus		Unknown	30
Follow me	Mrs. Bittle	J. H. Fillmore	87
For thee O dear, dear country	J. M. Neale, tr	J. P. Holbrook	71
From the cross uplifted high	T. Haweis	F. L. Armstrong	117
Glad and free	A. A. Hoskins	J. M. Stillman	38
Gloria Patri		Old English	3
Gloria in Excelsis Deo		"	5
Glory to the Father give		Hullah	120
God bless our native land	J. S. Dwight	A	135
God bless our school	A. Taylor	A. Taylor	7
God's free mercy streameth	H. P. Smith	Greek Hymn	31
God is love, his mercy brightens	J. Bowring	*	39
God my king thy might confessing	R. Mant	I. Conkey	30
Golden harps are sounding	F. R. Havergal	Perrina	20
Gracious Saviour, gentle shepherd	J. Whittemore	J	51
Greek Hymn	St. John of Damascus,	arr. J. P. H.	31
Growing up for Jesus	P. J. Owens	W. J. Kirkpatrick	110
Hark, hark, my soul angelic	F. W. Faber	H. Smart	65
Hark, the herald angels sing	Ch. Wesley	Mendelssohn	54
Hark, the voice of Jesus calling	Dr. March	P. P. Van Arsdale	45
He leadeth me	J. H. Gillmore,	arr. J. P. H.	23
Hear the pennies dropping	From Musical Herald		106
Heaven is our home	T. R. Taylor	A. S. Sullivan	67
Heavenly Father from thy throne		A. S. Sullivan	79

	AUTHOR.	COMPOSER OR SOURCE.	PAGE
Heavenly Father, hear our prayer	C. Malan, tr	◦	74
Heavenly Father, send thy blessing		H. Smart	138
He comes in blood-stained garments	Bancroft	English	43
He knoweth the way that I take	London Chris. World	J. P. Holbrook	76
Holy, holy, holy, Lord God Almighty	R. Heber	J. B. Dykes	8
Hosanna we sing		English	72
How firm a foundation, ye saints of	G. Keith	Reading	91
How gentle God's commands	P. Doddridge	Nageli	149
Hursley	J. Keble	W. H. Monk	12
Hushed was the evening hymn	J. D. Burns	A. S. Sullivan	140
I am little, but I love	J. E. Hall	J. E. Hall	114
I heard the voice of Jesus say	Bonar	Spohr	148
I left it all with Jesus	Helen H. Willis	English Melody	99
I love to tell the story	Miss Hankey	Fischer	63
I love to think of Heaven	W. Pearce	Beethoven	68
I love the holy angels		J. Stainer	62
I was a wandering sheep	Bonar	J. Zundel	92
I will not swear	From "Little Sower"	J. R. Murray	107
I would live like Jesus	S. S. Hymnal	E. P. Parker	96
In the cross of Christ I glory	J. Bowring	J. Conkey	128
In the King's army	E. E. Rexford	T. Martin Towne	46
In the vineyard of our Father	T. Mackellar	E. P. Parker	77
In the silent midnight watches	A. C. Coxe	G. F. Root	44
Is there one for me	Anon	arr. J. P. H.	33
It came upon the midnight clear	E. H. Sears	◦	61
It pays to do right	F. S. Pond	T. Martin Towne	142 & 143
Jerusalem the golden	J. Neale, tr	Ewing	70
Jesus Christ our Saviour	W. Whiting	◦	64
Jesus high in glory		T. R. Matthews	145
Jesus, I live to thee	H. Harbaugh	J. P. Holbrook	88
Jesus, I my cross have taken	H. F. Lyte	"	147
Jesus' little lamb am I		Geibel	111
Jesus loves me so	W. P. Smith	J. W. Pratt	112
Jesus, lover of my soul	Ch. Wesley	J. P. Holbrook	131
Jesus of Nazareth passeth by	Etta Campbell	arr. J. P. H.	25
Jesus, still lead on	Zinzendorf's Hymn	O. Drese	67
Jesus, thy name I love	H. F. Lyte	J. P. H.	149
Jewett	J. Borthwick, tr	Weber	134
Lead, kindly light	J. H. Newman	J. B. Dykes	49
Let the words of my mouth		Baumbach	6
Let us speak well of our brother		S. J. Vail	116
Little beams of brightness	W. Kibbey	J. H. Fillmore	106
Little children, come to Jesus			80
Little children pray	Mattie P. Smith	S. W. Straub	109
Little travelers Zionward	J. Edmeston	Unknown	125
Long ago in old Judea	Mrs. Bittle	J. H. Fillmore	87
Look, ye brothers	Luther James	T. Martin Towne	101
Love divine all love excelling	Ch. Wesley	J. Zundel	119
Lyte	H. F. Lyte	J. P. H.	149
Martyn	Ch. Wesley	Marsh	130
Mighty to save	R. W. Todd	H. Saunders	104
More love to thee	Mrs. Prentiss	J. P. H.	79
My ain countrie	Miss M. A. Lee	Scotch	36
My country, 'tis of thee	S. F. Smith	National Hymn	135
My days are gliding swiftly by	Dr. Nelson	G. F. Root	127
My God, my Father, while I stray	C. Elliott	Troyte Chant	18
My Jesus, as thou wilt	Schmolke	Weber	134
My spirit longs for thee	J. Byrom	Quartet & Cho. Choir	97
Nearer, my God, to thee	S. F. Adams	arr. L. Mason	129
Never alone	R. W. Raymond	F. Silcher	121
New every morning is the love	J. Keble	W. H. Monk	12
Now the day is over	S. B. Gould	J. Barnby	11
Now the shades of night are gone	Anon	Blumenthal	10
O blessed is that land	Chatterton Dix	arr. E. P. Parker	144
O come, let us sing unto the Lord	Bible	Chant	4
O day of rest and gladness	Wordsworth	German Mel.	154
O paradise, O paradise	Faber	J. Barnby	69
O the joy of calmly resting	J. W. S.	Geo. Speck	100
Once in royal David's city	C. F. Alexander	H. J. Gauntlet	57
One step more	S. S. Hymnal	E. P. Parker	29
One sweetly solemn thought	Miss Cary	J. P. H.	157
One there is above all others	J. Newton	"	41
Onward, Christian soldiers	S. B. Gould	Sullivan	16
Opening of school—Lord's prayer		Chant	3
Old hundred		M. Luther	13
Palms of glory, raiment bright	Montgomery	E. Ives	94
Praise God from whom all blessings flow		Luther	13
Praise, my soul, the king of Heaven	H. F. Lyte	J. P. Holbrook	66
Psalm of praise	F. S. Pierrepont	E. P. Parker	133

	AUTHOR.	COMPOSER OR SOURCE.	PAGE
Purer yet and purer	Anon	J. P. H.	35
Rejoice evermore	M. E. Servoss	A. Geibel	118
Rock of ages	Toplady	J. P. Holbrook	89
Saints in glory we together	S. E. Muhmied	German	22
Saviour, blessed Saviour	G. Thring	arr. J. P. H.	21
Saviour like a shepherd lead us	D. A. Thrupp	C. Steggall	146
Shepherd of thine Israel, lead us		J. Condar	146
Shining shore	Dr. Nelson	G. F. Root	127
Shout we with joy	W. C. Daland	W. C. Daland	136-137
Silent night, holy night	Anon		63
Sing evermore		Jas. Price	102
Sing to the King	M. Snodgrass	T. Martin Towne	113
Sing of Jesus, sing forever	T. Kelly	German	22
Singing on the way	M. E. Servoss	J. R. Sweeney	123
Sleep thy last sleep	E. A. Dayman	J. Barnby	156
Song of the little workers	Jessie Clement	J. McGranahan	78
Sons of Zion, raise your songs	T. Kelly	Hullah	120
Stand up, stand up for Jesus	Geo. Duffield	G. J. Webb	90
Star of Bethlehem	Happy voices	H. Kingsbury	52
Star of peace to wanderers weary	Simpson	J. P. H.	151
Sun of my soul, thou Saviour dear	J. Keble	W. H. Monk	12
Supplication	S. S. Hymnal	Sullivan	79
Sweet the moments, rich in blessing	Allen	J. Conkey	128
Tender Shepherd, thou hast stilled	C. Winkworth tr.	A. S. Sullivan	126
The better land	E. P. Parker	S. S. Hymnal	40
The day is past and over	J. M. Neale, tr	A. H. Brown	13
The gentle shepherd	M. G. Saffery	Thalberg	42
The golden ladder	N. Y. Observer	Beethoven	68
The Lord is my shepherd	Chant	L. Mason	7
The Lord's prayer		Tallis	3
The loving little ones	E. Unangst	Kurzenabbe	80
The morning light is breaking	S. F. Smith	G. J. Webb	90
The palace o' the King	W. Mitchell	J. J. Hood	37
The roseate hues of early dawn	C. F. Alexander	arr. German	153
The sweetest story	Mary B. Sleight	E. P. Parker	122
There is a beauty born of love	O. D. Sherman	J. M. Stillman	141
There is a green hill far away	C. F. Alexander	E. P. Parker	95
Those eternal bowers	St. John of Damascus	arr. J. P. H.	31
Thy way, not mine	F. Bonar	Weber	134
Thy will be done	J. Bowring	L. Mason	156
Too late	Tennyson	Lindsay	155
Toplady (Rock of ages)	Toplady	T. Hastings	88
Tranquil and peaceful	Anon	F. Flemming	75
Up yonder	Marg. Snodgrass	T. Martin Towne	103
Venite exultemus Domino		Old Chant	4
Waiting for Jesus	M. E. Servoss	G. C. Hugg	115
We are but little children weak	C. F. Alexander	C. E. Willing	108
We are but strangers here	T. R. Taylor	Sullivan	67
We are little pilgrims		Hullah	73
We are little students	Brainard Bros.	J. R. Murray	107
We are watching, we are waiting		G. F. Root	27
We march, we march to victory	G. Moultrie	J. Barnby	14 & 15
We plow the fields	J. Campbell, tr.	Schultz	84
We three kings of Orient are (Carol)	Hopkins	J. H. Hopkins	58
Weary of earth and laden with my sin	S. J. Stone	J. Langran	50
Welcome, happy morning	J. Ellerton	A. Sullivan	59
What a friend we have in Jesus	Bonar	J. P. Holbrook	41
What are these in bright array	Montgomery	E. Ives, jr	94
When his salvation bringing	J King	English	43
When the world is brightest	S. S. Hymnal	E. P. Parker	86
When thro' the torn sail	R Heber	Sullivan	151
Whiter than snow	J Nicholson	Fischer	48
Who is this that comes from Edom	E. P Parker	Ch. Guonod	93
Who loves the little children	H McE. Kimball	H. McE. Kimball	108
Words are things of little cost			86
Work, work, where shall we work	Mrs. Belle Towne	T. Martin Towne	82
Yield not to temptation	H. R. Palmer	H. R. Palmer	81

www.ingramcontent.com/pod-product-compliance
Lightning Source LLC
Chambersburg PA
CBHW020554270326

41927CB00006B/841